ENGLISH FOR INTERNATIONAL
TOURISM

T0346028

ANNA COWPER

CONTENTS

1 TOURISM TRENDS

UNIT MENU

Grammar: continuous aspect
Vocabulary: tourist motivations, describing statistics and visuals
Professional skills: using visuals
Case Study: tourism in India

1 Read the text about what motivates tourists. Match the sentences A–E with the gaps 1–5.

Many of the reasons that motivate people to travel have remained the same throughout history. It has always been the case, for example, that people will travel to see family and friends.[1]____
Many of the earliest travellers were pilgrims seeking to improve their health, either by visiting a shrine or other holy place, or, like some early Roman tourists, hoping to cure their rheumatism by bathing in hot springs. [2]____ A further significant and unchanging motivation for travel is the spirit of curiosity and the quest for adventure that motivated explorers such as Columbus and Marco Polo.[3]____ People have also always tended to use travel experiences as a way to impress each other and acquire prestige.

[4]____However, as leisure time increases and pursuits that were once only available to the privileged few are enjoyed by the masses, modern tourists are increasingly attracted by anything authentic they can feel a part of – 'the real Greece', or 'authentic Spain'. [5]____ According to travel researcher A. Barlow, 'What captivates the modern traveller is the idea that this mountain, this view of the sea, takes me outside my ordinary experience: it is precious in its uniqueness and fulfilling in a way that makes me more than I was.' Those tourism providers who understand this need and can find ways to meet it are those that will prosper most in the future.

A They have become acquirers and collectors of experiences, a phenomenon known as 'the experience economy'.

B Nowadays, people routinely travel round the world to visit their children or grandchildren, or perhaps a best friend who's got a new job in a different country.

C These days, this finds its expression in extreme sports or adventure holidays in exotic places, such as trekking in the Amazon jungle or climbing in the Himalayas.

D This is mirrored today in the renewed popularity of spa breaks and a wide range of different kinds of health and wellness vacations, from medical tourism to yoga and meditation holidays.

E For example, going on certain kinds of expensive holiday, such as a luxury cruise, is a way in which the socially ambitious can affirm their wealth and status.

2 Complete the table with the missing nouns, verbs or adjectives. You will find most of them in the text. Use a dictionary to help as needed.

Noun	Verb	Adjective
ambition		1 _____
2 _____	3 _____	acquisitive
4 _____	fulfil	5 _____
6 _____	motivation	7 _____
8 _____		prestigious
prosperity	9 _____	10 _____

3 Complete the sentences with the correct form of words in the table.

1 The need to collect experiences could be seen as a typically _____ urge of our consumer society.

2 People go on spa breaks to _____ their need to recover from a stressful lifestyle.

3 Luxury cruises are expensive and beyond the reach of all but the most _____ tourists.

4 People gain status by doing something that others cannot: the more exclusive the experience, the more _____ it is.

5 The idea that they are doing exactly the same thing as everyone else isn't _____ for most modern tourists.

4)))) 1.1   Listen to three people – Marc, Sharon and Andrei – talking about their holidays as a child and the kinds of vacation they take now. Who mentions each of these things? Write M, S or A.

adrenalin _____   problems with unfamiliar food _____   the Sahara desert _____
ancient ruins _____   working parents _____   activities for children _____
sunburn _____   stress _____   youth camps _____

5 Listen again and complete the summaries of how the people's holiday experiences have changed.

- As a child, Marc never travelled very much but spent most of his holidays with his ¹_____ in the South of France. Nowadays, he has very ²_____ holiday time but travels widely. He enjoys ³_____ sports and intense experiences.
- Sharon used to go on ⁴_____ holidays to Spain and Greece with her parents. Nowadays, she prefers not to travel ⁵_____ with her young family and instead likes to ⁶_____ a holiday home by the sea in the UK.
- When Andrei was growing up, there were few ⁷_____ for international travel, so now he loves to travel abroad. For Andrei and his wife, ⁸_____ is very important when they travel, so they enjoy package tours to European ⁹_____ .

6 Choose the correct option to complete the sentences about the development of the luxury travel market.

1 Nowadays, Thailand and South Africa have become mainstream destinations, ideal for adventurous travellers who *are / were* looking for new exotic places to explore.

2 Over the last few years, the Russian Far East and Greenland *have been / are* developing their tourism facilities in response to new interest from American tourists.

3 New destinations *are being / are* opened up in places that were formerly resistant to tourism, such as Bhutan and Cambodia.

4 In the past, local stakeholders may have felt that they *were being / have been being* exploited by tourism developers, but there are more positive feelings about these latest initiatives.

5 Exclusive cultural tourism is an area which many tourism providers *have been / will be* investing in recently, and lots of interesting new products *are / were* appearing on the market.

6 Due to its prohibitive cost, it is unlikely that space tourism *will be / will have* expanded significantly by the year 2050.

PRONUNCIATION

7)))) 1.2   The *-ing* sound in a verb is always unstressed but must be pronounced. Listen and choose the word or phrase in each pair that you hear. Note the stressed syllable.

1 seeing – sing   3 calling – call in   5 ringing – ring in

2 coming – come in   4 bringing – bring in   6 looking – look in

8)))) 1.3   Listen and repeat the pairs of words/phrases.

TOURISM TRENDS

1))) **1.4**   Listen to a UK travel representative talking about the growth of the grey market tourism sector in the UK. What reason is given for the UK's popularity with senior travellers?

2 **Listen again. Are the statements true (T) or false (F)?**

1 Last year, one in four visitors to the UK was in the over-55 age group.   T/F

2 In 1993, one out of every eight visitors to the UK was a grey traveller.   T/F

3 British ex-pats are the second largest group of grey visitors to the UK.   T/F

4 There will be 100,000 more Chinese visitors to the UK by 2014.   T/F

5 Young people rank the UK third on the list of countries they would visit if money were no object.   T/F

6 Grey travellers don't like too much special attention.   T/F

3 **Circle the word in each group that has a different meaning from the others.**

1 slightly / (by) a little / considerably / somewhat

2 increase / rise / go up / grow / level off / expand / boost

3 surge / soar / rise / drop / swell / go up

4 dip / fall / decrease / surge / go down / drop / decline

5 slump / crash / collapse / grow / plummet

6 sharply / abruptly / dramatically / gently / suddenly

4 **Rewrite the sentences so that they have a similar meaning, replacing the words in bold with words with a similar meaning. There is more than one possible answer.**

1 The number of inbound visits **soared** when the UK hosted the Olympic Games.

2 The overall growth of the market **dipped slightly** from 2008 to 2010 due to the economic recession.

3 Fuel prices **fell a little**, which has made it possible for low-cost carriers to lower their fares.

4 Visitor numbers **slumped dramatically** in the first quarter of the year due to bad weather.

5 Grey tourism is predicted to **increase** steadily in the UK.

5 **Look at the visuals below and read the beginning of a presentation about tourism growth in India. Complete the text with the words and phrases in the box.**

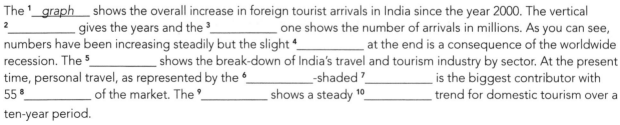

  axis   bar chart   black   dip   ~~graph~~   horizontal   percent   pie chart   segment   upward

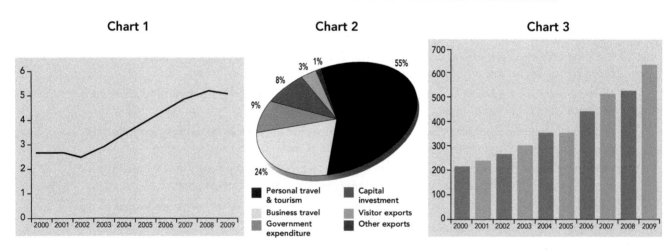

Chart 1   **Chart 2**   **Chart 3**

Chart 2 legend: Personal travel & tourism; Business travel; Government expenditure; Capital investment; Visitor exports; Other exports

The **1** _graph_ shows the overall increase in foreign tourist arrivals in India since the year 2000. The vertical **2**_____ gives the years and the **3**_____ one shows the number of arrivals in millions. As you can see, numbers have been increasing steadily but the slight **4**_____ at the end is a consequence of the worldwide recession. The **5**_____ shows the break-down of India's travel and tourism industry by sector. At the present time, personal travel, as represented by the **6**_____-shaded **7**_____ is the biggest contributor with 55 **8**_____ of the market. The **9**_____ shows a steady **10**_____ trend for domestic tourism over a ten-year period.

1 Read the report about how India is developing as a tourist destination. Choose the correct option, a, b, or c, for each gap.

India's tourism future

In the 1960s and 70s, many Western tourists to India were students and ¹____ who travelled in search of spiritual enlightenment or cultural discovery. This group travelled light on ²____ budgets and their contribution in terms of revenue to their host country was limited. Forty years ³____, the situation has changed dramatically. Today India is one of the ⁴____ world tourism destinations, with its foreign exchange from tourism ⁵____ to show an annual growth of 14% over the next four years. This turnaround is a result of several factors, not least India's high ⁶____ in world affairs due to its economic achievements. The tourism industry searches constantly for new destinations to promote and develop and the Indian government's national tourism promotion campaign 'Incredible India' has proved very successful in raising India's global ⁷____. Although internal infrastructure continues to be a ⁸____ , investment in transport links and hotels is ongoing as the Indian tourism industry ⁹____ and develops. New and developing areas include eco-tourism, a flourishing medical tourism sector and new ¹⁰____ sectors, such as golf tourism and tea tourism.

1	**a** walkers	**b** backpackers	**c** hikers
2	**a** restricted	**b** restrained	**c** constricted
3	**a** after	**b** later	**c** further
4	**a** fast-moving	**b** faster growing	**c** fastest-growing
5	**a** believed	**b** forecast	**c** reminded
6	**a** visibility	**b** presence	**c** success
7	**a** face	**b** profile	**c** influence
8	**a** lack	**b** insufficiency	**c** weakness
9	**a** matures	**b** ages	**c** produces
10	**a** special	**b** obscure	**c** niche

2 Complete the information about the Indian outbound travel market with the words and figures in the boxes.

> boom   campaigns   proximity   second   socio-economic   VFR

> 25–65   3.7   1,850,000   40%

The Indian outbound travel market has grown from around ¹_____ million in 1977 to an expected 11–13 million this year. In percentage terms, it is now the fastest-growing market in the world and in terms of numbers, it's the ²_____ fastest after China.

In response to the ³_____ many countries – including Ireland, Spain, South Korea and Poland – have opened tourist offices in India. Many others offer packages and run ⁴_____ specifically directed at the Indian tourist.

⁵_____ of all outbound trips by Indians are for business purposes, while leisure, visiting friends and relatives (⁶_____) and other reasons each account for 20% of outbound trips from India.

International Indian tourists are generally ⁷_____ years of age, a larger proportion being males (65%) than females (35%). They are well-educated and belong to the upper ⁸_____ strata of society. The majority are married (75%) and two-thirds of leisure travellers tend to holiday abroad with their family.

Countries such as Malaysia, Thailand and Singapore remain the most preferred destinations, due to their ⁹_____and cheaper costs. However, Western cities, especially New York and London, are extremely popular destinations. In 2010, London had almost 250,000 Indian visitors and New York had ¹⁰_____, a 26% increase on the previous year.

2 GET THE MESSAGE

UNIT MENU

Grammar: countable and uncountable nouns
Vocabulary: advertising and publicity, web words, collocations
Professional skills: maintaining a website
Case study: improve a company website

1 Javier Alvarez and Scott Jackson's start-up Adventure North offers kayaking and backpacking packages in the Canadian wilderness. Choose the correct option to complete the extract from the brief to the website designer.

Technical information

- It must be possible to display the site using different web ¹*browsers / searchers / engines* on different devices. We predict that our future customers are going to be ²*subscribing / accessing / following* websites via their smartphones. It is important that the quality of the experience is the same whether the site is ³*viewed / watched / looked* from the larger screen of a PC or from a laptop.

- Following our discussion, we decided to restrict ourselves to PayPal as the ⁴*reservation / payment / updating* system for online bookings.

- It is essential that the ⁵*navigation / searching / routing* of the site is as straightforward as possible. We would like a very simple home page, with ⁶*checks / posts / links* to all other parts of the site from it.

Look and feel

- We want to use the site to help create a dynamic ⁷*media / product / brand* image for the company that's going to ⁸*attract / appeal / advance* to Adventure North's client profile. Our target market is urban professionals from their mid-20s to early 50s, affluent, interested in sports, fitness, nature and outdoor pursuits.

- We attach a folder with samples of colours, logos and house style in the brief. We are looking for a simple, 'clean', ⁹*unconventional / untidy / uncluttered* look without, for example, lots of different ¹⁰*letter / font / alphabet* styles. We will also supply you with a portfolio of photos.

2))) **2.1** Javier phones Megan Reid at Creative Communications to give some initial feedback on the website design. Listen to the conversation and tick (✓) the THREE main problems.

☐ ugly graphics   ☐ drop-down menus not visible without a mouse over

☐ fonts too small   ☐ colours too bright and childish

☐ inappropriate sound effects   ☐ too much scrolling down needed

☐ drop-down menus don't work   ☐ long loading time

3 Listen again and complete the phrases with ONE to THREE words.

1 Javier thinks the _____ look cool.

2 Some of the graphics looked a bit ugly in the samples, but they work really well _____ .

3 The version of the home page with the sound effects just _____ to load.

4 Megan thinks that perhaps there is a problem with the _____ in the version she sent.

5 Javier and Scott would prefer their clients to be able to see the drop-down menus _____ .

6 They'd like the menu to be visible without having to _____ or mouse over anything.

7 Javier asks Megan to take the fonts up a _____ .

8 Scott wants there to be a link through to his expedition blog from _____ .

4 Complete the article about the benefits of social media sites with the words in the box.

> coverage   credible   hosted   mouse   networks   posting   shoestring   viral

Why your tourism business needs social media

OK, so social media isn't all good news but if your company has a social media policy in place, you'll have the resources to respond to that bad review on TripAdvisor immediately, before it has time to impact on your business. You can do this very effectively, too because the amazing power of social media lies in the amount of ¹_____ it gives you. Because social networks are ²_____ , a video or a tweet can be viewed by millions within just a few hours of its ³_____ . Two-thirds of the global internet population visit social ⁴_____ and this means you can get your messages out to your customers faster than you could possibly have imagined and all on just a ⁵_____ budget. You get your customers to do the work for you. Not only that but if, for example, your video is ⁶_____ by a site such as Youtube, you don't have to worry much about the technical side of things either. As people become increasingly tired of the hard sell, the personalized nature of a social media message is more ⁷_____ than traditional advertising. These days, getting your message across by 'word of ⁸_____ ' is not only the quickest but also the most effective way of winning your customers' hearts and minds.

5 Choose the best answer to complete the sentences.

1 We asked the designer for _____ but she was reluctant to give us any.

  a an advice   **b** some pieces of advice   **c** some advice   **d** a piece of advice

2 The woman in the tourist office gave us two _____ .

  a information   **b** pieces of information   **c** lots of information   **d** informations

3 _____ is there available for this project? It's going to be expensive.

  a How much money   **b** How many moneys   **c** How much moneys   **d** How many moneys

4 _____ are we talking about in terms of initial investment?

  a How many   **b** How much   **c** How big   **d** How often

5 We'll send you a draft proposal and then I suggest you give us _____ on our initial ideas.

  a a feedback   **b** feedbacks   **c** some feedback   **d** some feedbacks

6 I think the problem is that we haven't really done _____ for this product.

  a any promotion   **b** a promotion   **c** any promotions   **d** promotions

7 How many _____ do we need for each for each person? They need to make notes.

  a papers   **b** paper   **c** pieces of papers   **d** pieces of paper

8 He has very _____ of working directly with clients. He's not the best person for the job.

  a few experience   **b** little experience   **c** much experience   **d** a lot of experience

GET THE MESSAGE

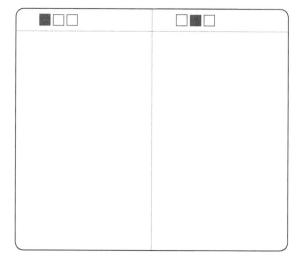

Social Media

1 Scott Jackson has asked Megan Reid of Creative Communications for some advice about increasing traffic to the Adventure North blog. Read her email reply. Correct the <u>underlined</u> factual mistakes.

Hi Scott

You'll be happy to know that increasing traffic to your blog isn't difficult. This might seem obvious but the essential thing is delivering killer content! So, be clever, be funny, ask questions and tell interesting stories. You should also do at least some of the following:

1 Remember that people want you to talk about them not you, so write in the <u>first</u> person ('you' not 'me').

2 Link to other sites that appeal to <u>a different audience from</u> the one you are trying to reach.

3 Connect with other bloggers. Guest-post on someone else's blog. Post <u>negative</u> comments on other high-quality blogs you come across.

4 Search engine optimization (SEO) is vital – this means creating content that is found more easily by <u>browsers</u>, such as Google.

5 Use a linkback method, such as Trackback, to request notification when somebody <u>looks at</u> any of your content. This enables you to keep track of who isn't linking to your blog.

6 If you are prepared to spend some money to increase your traffic, look into paid keywords schemes, such as Google Adwords. It's <u>cheap</u> but worth it as it's a good way to drive instant targeted traffic to your site.

Cheers

Meg

---

2 Look at the booking terms and conditions on Adventure North's website. Match the beginnings 1–6 with the endings a–f.

1 A non-refundable, non-transferrable deposit of 50%

2 Your reservation will be automatically cancelled

3 You must ensure all names and details

4 Final payment is due 45

5 Changes and cancellations to all or part of a booking

6 We cannot accept responsibility if we are not notified of inaccuracies within

a days prior to departure.

b are subject to amendment and cancellation fees.

c are entered correctly at the time of booking.

d of the total costs is payable on booking.

e eight days of sending out the invoice.

f if your deposit is not received by the due date.

3 Circle the word that CANNOT be used with the verb in bold on the left.

1 **post:** content / comments / photos / traffic / updates

2 **click on:** a link / an icon / a server / a drop-down menu

3 **subscribe to:** a newsletter / an update service / your customers / Facebook / Twitter

4 **host:** a file / a guest blogger / a menu

5 **embed:** videos / podcasts / links / robots / keywords

6 **optimize:** a search engine / your contact list / a cursor / your social media profile

PRONUNCIATION

4 Put the words in the box into the correct group according to their stress pattern.

---

amendment   audience   correctly
customers   easily   enables   essential
increasing   negative   newsletter
remember   targeted

■□□	□■□

5))) 2.2 Listen and check your answers. Then listen and repeat.

1 Numbers have been falling at Pilgrim Camps adventure holidays for 14- to17-year-olds. The new managing director, Morley Johnson, has asked for help from media consultants. Read the extracts from a report and an email and complete them with the words in the box.

> comments   developers   exiting   features
> Google   optimization   logging on
> social media

If you share great content about topics related to your organization on ¹_____ platforms as well as on your company website, you'll get more hits from users and, thanks to these, higher rankings on ²_____ and other search engines. We need to work on search engine ³_____ as a matter of priority. Your young customers are likely to enjoy connecting with each other via Facebook posts and tweets and by leaving ⁴_____ on review sections, etc. So your site needs to link in with popular social networking sites.

I'm sorry, Morley, you've got what my old boss would have called a 'Frankenstein site'. It looks as if the company has just added new ⁵_____ in a random, haphazard way over a number of years using different ⁶_____, so the result is, frankly, a bit of a mess. It's no surprise that your mobile users are ⁷_____ the site an average of five seconds after ⁸_____ ! It's bad code on top of bad code and I think it might be best to scrap this site and start again from scratch.

2 Read the texts again and answer the questions.

   1 Which text is about:
     a the company's website?   **b** its social media profile?

   2 Which text is from:
     a someone Morley knows well?   **b** a professional media consultant?

   3 Why is the company website in such a bad state?

   4 How does having a social media profile help with search engine optimization?

3))) 2.3 Listen to Morley's meeting with Georgia, the marketing director. Are the statements below true (T) or false (F)?

   1 Pilgrims target customers who don't use social media very much.   T/F

   2 There are security issues attached to social media used by children.   T/F

   3 Georgia suggests that Facebook content should be kept separate from the website.   T/F

   4 Georgia thinks that Pilgrims should use social media to tell stories about what happens at their camps.   T/F

   5 Morley isn't worried that the use of social media might have negative consequences.   T/F

   6 Georgia believes that it is possible to turn even bad reviews to your advantage.   T/F

4 Match the words and expressions 1–6 (which are all from this spread) with the definitions a–f.

   1 browser   **a** the computer data and instructions which determine on-screen content

   2 build up traffic   **b** to put text, photos or other content on a social media site

   3 code   **c** to increase the number of people visiting a site

   4 guest-post   **d** a piece of software that runs on your PC and lets you access webpages

   5 post   **e** a Facebook function of embedding links in a photo to identify the people shown in it and link through to their profiles

   6 tagging   **f** to contribute content to someone else's blog

3 HOTEL BRANDING

UNIT MENU

Grammar: making predictions
Vocabulary: brands, hotel facilities, financial terms
Professional skills: creating a business plan
Case study: invest in a hotel

1 **Read about three fashionable boutique hotels in New York City. Which hotel or hotels:**

1 used to be an industrial building?

2 is in an area that used to be poor and rough?

3 is associated with a particular period in history?

4 has a pool?

5 offers free food?

6 is associated with culture and the arts?

The Chattanooga

Small but exquisite, this <u>intimate</u> 25-room luxury boutique hotel in New York's theatre district gives guests a taste of the glamour of the 1920s and the age of jazz. Formerly home to society hostess Helena Carson, who used to entertain writers such as F. Scott Fitzgerald in her <u>sophisticated</u> salon, the building has been lovingly restored and preserves all its original Art Deco elegance. The opulent period décor of the bedrooms is complemented by playful 1920s touches such as Bauhaus-style chairs and lamps and reproductions of period magazines and newspapers.

The Spice House

This SoHo boutique hotel is located in a former spice warehouse and embodies the hip, creative neighbourhood it inhabits. With over 400 original works of art on display on the walls, guests can experience the SoHo scene without leaving the hotel, especially since the helpful, <u>attentive</u> staff even includes a hotel art curator. The loft-style guest rooms are ultra-modern but stylish and <u>aesthetically-pleasing</u> and are full of thoughtful details such as a customized selection of bedside reading books and magazines. In addition, there is an arts café with a stunning rooftop terrace overlooking central Manhattan which holds regular arts events and gastronomic evenings with 'tasters' for all on the house.

East is East

East is East is <u>immaculate</u> in every respect, from its beautiful interior to all the extras on offer, such as a complimentary gym pass, and free DVD and Wii rentals. Despite its location in East Village, New York's former skid row, the spirit of East is East is high-tech luxury with an oriental touch. All the rooms have floor-to-ceiling windows and come equipped with iPads from which guests can do everything from ordering room service to controlling the lighting. While many hotels of this size (88 guest rooms) don't have much when it comes to on-site <u>amenities</u>, East is East has an underground pool, a spa and an excellent gym.

2 **Complete the sentences with the underlined words in the texts.**

1 People expect particularly _____ service and a greater degree of attention to detail from a boutique hotel.

2 The hotel has been decorated by world-class designers in a _____ contemporary style.

3 Although built of concrete, the building is elegant and _____ , with its curved white walls and glass roof.

4 The place has been cleaned from top to bottom and entirely refurbished: it's now _____ .

5 The soft lighting and individual booths give the restaurant a cosy and _____ feel.

6 The hotel was small but the _____ were first class.

3 **Match the beginnings of 1–5 with endings a–e to make sentences about how hotels build their brand.**

1 Since competing on price isn't a good strategy in the hospitality industry,

2 Hotels develop brands by tailoring what they offer

3 Brands are designed to communicate a particular set of associations or values

4 Brand awareness is created

5 It is also essential to create brand loyalty

a through carefully targeted advertising and marketing.

b by consistently delivering the same calibre of experience, so that guests will keep returning.

c which the target customer will identify with and share.

d hotels have to find a variety of ways to distinguish themselves from their competitors.

e to meet the specific budget, travel and lifestyle requirements of their target customer profile.

4 **Put the expressions in the box into the correct place according to the degree of certainty they express.**

> bound to ~~could~~ is very likely to may might the chances are that the likelihood is that will definitely will probably

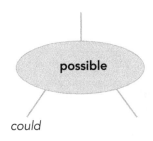

(almost certain)

(very possible)

(possible)

could

5))) 3.1 **Alison Saunders from *Hotel* magazine is interviewing Chuck Pinto of Fast Futures Research about the hotels of the future. Listen and tick (✓) the things below that are mentioned.**

☐ space hotels
☐ robot room cleaning
☐ disposable bed linen
☐ underwater hotels
☐ increased personalization
☐ face-recognition systems
☐ robot room service
☐ lower staffing levels
☐ high technology costs

6 **Complete the predictions with an expression from Exercise 4. There is sometimes more than one possible answer. Then listen to the interview again and check the predictions the speakers used.**

1 Hotels on the moon or under the sea _____ exist very soon.

2 Technology _____ play a significant part in the way hotels evolve.

3 Since staff functions are going to be replaced by computers, _____ hotels will be staffed by fewer people in the future.

4 Receptionists' jobs _____ be the first to disappear.

5 The whole checking-in process _____ very soon be a thing of the past.

6 In the near future, some companies _____ start using robots instead of humans to clean rooms.

7 Despite the fact that there will be fewer staff, _____ the hotel experience will be more personalized in the future, not less.

8 Alison predicts that there are _____ be technical problems with all these new systems.

9 Chuck thinks that small hotels _____ find it difficult to meet the costs of maintaining all the systems.

1 Look at the DOs and DON'Ts for writing a business plan. Complete the sentences by crossing out the incorrect DO/DON'T and using a word from the box in each gap.

> experience   financial   niche   promotion   revenues   risks   skills   threats

DOs AND DON'Ts FOR WRITING A HOTEL BUSINESS PLAN

DO / DON'T describe yourself, your team and your previous ¹_____ .

DO / DON'T forget how much you will have to spend on ²_____ and advertising in the first year.

DO / DON'T make the business plan too long and repetitive.

DO / DON'T state who your hotel will cater for and define your ³_____ .

DO / DON'T be over-optimistic – investors will probably cut your estimated ⁴_____ by half anyway.

DO / DON'T show how you intend to advertise and promote the business.

DO / DON'T outline the strengths, weaknesses, opportunities and ⁵_____ to your venture.

DO / DON'T provide the necessary ⁶_____ information.

DO / DON'T undersell yourself – you need to come across as someone who has the necessary ⁷_____ .

DO / DON'T hide the potential ⁸_____ that you run; investors like to be prepared for what these might be.

2 Match the financial terms 1–8 with the definitions a–h.

1 fee		**a**	a summary of how much money a company has and how much it owes
2 budget		**b**	you have this if you spend more money than your bank account contains
3 overheads		**c**	the money that a company earns from its business activities
4 rate		**d**	money you borrow from the bank to finance buying a property
5 revenue		**e**	ongoing costs from operating a business, e.g. rent for the building
6 balance sheet		**f**	payment for professional advice or services
7 overdraft		**g**	the amount you charge for a service
8 mortgage		**h**	a future plan for how you intend to manage and spend money

3))) 3.2   Michael and Sally Gamble aren't sure what room rates to charge at their newly opened Bed & Breakfast. Listen to their meeting with their accountant and answer the questions.

1 How many rooms do they have?

2 The factors that the accountant suggest they use to calculate the room rate are:
number of bed _____ and rate of _____ .

4 Listen again and complete the information about the room rates they should charge.

Start-up costs = _____ euros + desired return on investment = _____ euros

Worst case scenario

Target sales revenue = 60,000 euros ÷ _____ bed nights sold = Room rate of _____ euros

Better case scenario

Target sales revenue = 60,000 euros ÷ _____ bed nights sold = Room rate of _____ euros

1 Naomi Chen is considering investing in a luxury boutique hotel in Guangzhou in China. She has asked for some advice form Lu Jin at Hotel Solutions. Read the email reply and circle the best options.

From:	Jin@hotelsolutions.com
To:	naomichen@j.mail.com
Subject:	hotel advice

Naomi

I thought that the ¹*property / premise / place*, you showed me, the former monastery by the lake, was stunningly beautiful and I loved your concept but you do need to be aware of the risks. It's true that your target market of customers in their early 20s to mid-50s with mid- to upper- ²*wages / fees / incomes* is growing fast in Guangzhou but the competition for this market segment is intense. The ³*up / high / rich*-end of the hotel sector is expanding fast, but the occupancy rate at high-⁴*marking / ranking / scoring* hotels in the province was a little more than 60% in the final quarter of last year. As you know, a hotel barely breaks ⁵*even / flat / out* if the rate is lower than 60%.

On the other hand, if you take the independent route, you won't have to pay a franchise ⁶*fee / cost / price* to become part of a larger ⁷*chain / set / line* and you can survive and succeed without the costly ⁸*amenities / premises / equipment,* such as ballrooms and meeting spaces, that the city hotels have to offer. Actually, I think your biggest problem might be finding the right staff. Personalized ⁹*attentive / focused / concentrated* service is what distinguishes boutique hotels from the mainstream, but what hoteliers in Guangzhou are finding is that the most talented people get snapped up by five-star hotels run by big international brands which can offer attractive ¹⁰*fees / expenses / salaries.*

Anyway, these are just some initial reactions. Looking forward to talking more next week.

All best wishes

Jin

2 Read the text again. In what ways would the five-star hotels in the city be a threat to Naomi's business?

3))) 3.3 Lu Jin has an alternative business proposition for Naomi. Listen to their conversation and answer the questions.

    1 What does Lu Jin propose as an alternative to investing in a boutique hotel?

    2 She suggests Naomi should meet Michael Yu – what is his job?

4 Listen again. Are the statements true (T) or false (F)?

    1 Naomi isn't sure that her concept would fit with the Golden Dragon.   T/F

    2 The main advantage of Lu Jin's proposition would be the immediate visibility of the hotel in the market.   T/F

    3 Naomi's initial start-up expenses would be smaller.   T/F

    4 The only financial disadvantage of the scheme would be the ongoing royalty Naomi would pay.   T/F

    5 Lu Jin agrees that the initial promotional spend would be substantial but worth the investment.   T/F

    6 Naomi needs to find out more about all the Golden Dragon's brand policies.   T/F

PRONUNCIATION

5))) 3.4 Listen and write the three numbers in the order you hear them.

    1 16,000   60,000   600,000

    2 40,000   14,000   1.4

    3 12,000   120,000   12,000,000

    4 700,000   17,000   70,000

    5 90,000   19,000   9.19

    6 18,000   88,000   80,000

6 Listen again and repeat.

4 SUSTAINABILITY

UNIT MENU

Grammar: reporting verbs
Vocabulary: positive and negative connotations
Professional skills: chairing a meeting
Case study: assess impact of tourism on a fragile environment

1 Read about tourism development in Dubai. Complete the gaps in the text with the best option, a, b or c.

1 a spent	**b** invested	**c** bought
2 a fencing off	**b** siphoning off	**c** raking off
3 a brand	**b** label	**c** mark
4 a promotion	**b** policy	**c** campaign
5 a fake	**b** synthetic	**c** artificial
6 a resort	**b** campus	**c** centre
7 a placement	**b** location	**c** site
8 a donated	**b** subsidised	**c** contributed

Sunshine and shopping in Dubai: an economic success story

Over the last 20 years, the government of Dubai has ¹_____ heavily in tourism infrastructure by ²_____ money from its diminishing oil revenues into ambitious real-estate projects, such as the construction of the ultra-luxurious Burj-Al-Arab (opened in 1999), the world's first seven-star hotel. As well as pouring money into high-end, opulent hotels, Dubai has transformed itself into a shoppers' paradise, constructing lavishly-decorated shopping malls with ³_____-name shops and entertainment complexes.

To complete the new image, the government launched a global media ⁴_____ featuring images of falcons hunting in the desert and tourists relaxing on sunlit beaches to promote Dubai as a resort, while simultaneously spending billions of dollars creating ⁵_____ beaches with sand and rocks dredged from the Arabian Gulf. The construction of the Palm Islands, an entire ⁶_____ complete with hotels, shops and luxury apartments and built on a specially constructed archipelago of islands off its coast, was the jewel in the crown. Dubai's sunny climate, as well as its strategic ⁷_____ between Asia and Europe within a non-stop flight from almost all major cities, have ⁸_____ to its appeal, particularly for winter holidaymakers and have helped to make Dubai's reinvention of itself as a sunshine and shopping holiday resort one of the tourism success stories of the 21st century.

2))) 4.1 Listen to Abdul Rhaman bin Fahd from the Dubai School of Tourism talking about sustainable development. Why was Dubai so badly hit by the economic crisis of 2008?

3 Listen again and complete the sentences with up to THREE words.

1 Certain changes need to be made to Dubai's tourism industry in order for it to be _____ .

2 Dubai can't offer much in the way of historic or _____ .

3 We have world-class amenities, but we need to leverage them to target a wider _____ .

4 We could repurpose some of our existing hotels to focus on family tourism and to _____ .

5 We have proposed creating transport connections between Dubailand and _____ .

6 Most importantly of all, we believe that Dubai's tourism industry needs more _____ .

4 Group the factors in the box according to whether the negative impact they have on tourism development is mainly social, economic or environmental.

> air and water pollution   leakage of profits   loss of culture   low 'local' wages in tourism jobs
> over-dependence on tourism of local economy   problems with sewage/waste disposal
> property price increases   rise in crime levels   soil erosion
> tension between local tourism providers and multinationals   threats to local wildlife
> visitors outnumber locals   water shortages

negative
social
impacts

negative
economic
impacts

negative
environmental
impacts

5))) 4.2   Leroy, Doris and Carlton are talking about how tourism has changed their African island. Complete the conversation with the correct form of appropriate words from Exercise 4. Then listen and check your answers.

Doris: OK, I admit that there are jobs now but what kind of jobs? It's OK if you want to earn local ¹_____ as a bartender but at management level, foreigners ²_____ locals by ten to one at least – that's not fair! All the real profit ³_____ away back to the multinational providers.

Leroy: What worries me most is the environmental damage, especially to the coral reefs, caused by water ⁴_____ . Some of the hotels have problems with ⁵_____ disposal and they illegally dump it in the sea.

Carlton: No, that's simply not true anymore, Leroy! Have you forgotten about all the new regulations in place to protect local plants and ⁶_____ ? Most hotels now have recycling programmes to help manage their ⁷_____ . As for getting a better job, Doris, why don't you try and improve your qualifications like I did?

Leroy: But, come on, Carlton, look at what's happened to local ⁸_____ prices – a house on the waterfront can sell for a million dollars now. It's not surprising that ⁹_____ rates and violence have risen in the downtown tourist area and it's going to get worse, you mark my words. ¹⁰_____ is growing between the police and the street gangs.

Carlton: OK, it's true that development brings its own problems but you can't stop progress!

6 Complete the account of the conversation in Exercise 5 with the reporting verbs in the box.

> acknowledged   agreed   complained   denied   reminded   suggested   told   warned

1 Doris _____ that the tourism industry had created jobs on the island but she _____ that all the management level jobs have been taken by non-locals.

2 Leroy _____ the others that his greatest worry was pollution.

3 Carlton _____ the fact that hotels were still pumping sewage into the sea.

4 He _____ Leroy and Doris about the new regulations in place to protect the environment.

5 Carlton _____ that Doris should try to improve her qualifications if she wants a better job.

6 Leroy _____ the others that crime was going to get worse.

7 Carlton _____ that tourism development had brought problems as well as benefits but said that it was useless to try to stop progress.

PRONUNCIATION

7))) 4.3   For each group of words, underline the word which contains the short form of the vowel. Listen and check your answers.

1 leak   reach   sit   meet

2 mark   arm   plant   brand

3 short   sport   hot   warn

4 each   reef   still   mean

5 palm   part   back   dark

6 more   what   bought   salt

7 gang   range   state   stage

8 food   book   new   too

1)) **4.4** Listen to the conversation between two colleagues, Anja and Solomon, about a meeting. What was the meeting supposed to be about? What did the participants spend most of the time discussing?

2 Choose the best answer to summarize Anja's account of the meeting. Then listen again and check.

1 The minutes of the meeting **a** were incomplete **b** haven't been circulated yet **c** were circulated late.

2 a All **b** Not many **c** Most of the essential decisions were made.

3 By lunchtime they had covered **a** all **b** most **c** some of the agenda

4 The meeting was **a** longer **b** more interesting **c** more important than Anja expected.

5 a Anja **b** Jeremy **c** Barnaby dominated the discussion.

6 Anja thinks that the chair is **a** not strict enough **b** too strict **c** in control as regards people digressing.

3 Put the words in order to make eight expressions which are useful for chairing meetings. Some are statements and some are questions.

1 come / anyone / to / here / in / Does / want

_____

2 under / we / stick / the / discussion / Can / point / to

_____

3 so / I / we're / all / think / shall / started / here, / get / we

_____

4 anyone / add / have / that /anything / Does / to / to

_____

5 agenda / and / afraid / we're / of time / we / I'm / really must / the / running out / keep to

_____

6 there / anyone / further / raise / points / any / wants to / Are

_____

7 next / on / item / to / the / on / the / Let's / agenda / move

_____

8 come / we / later / could / to / Perhaps / back / that

_____

4 Match the expressions 1–8 in Exercise 3 with their purpose a–d.

a Beginning the meeting ____

b Inviting participants to contribute ____ ____ ____

c Moving on to a new area of the discussion ____

d Dealing with digressions – bringing the discussion back to the main point ____ ____ ____

5 Proofread the minutes of a meeting. Find and correct FOUR spelling, TWO punctuation and TWO grammar mistakes.

National Park Conservation Committee Meeting

Time: 14 September, 10.30–12.00   **Venu:** Meeting Room 2   **Present:** AH, JM, BL, SP, JJ

1 Visitor numbers

Numbers are up 40% since the opening of the new visitors' centre. Bearing in mind the growing numbers of visitors from China, SP suggested that we should provide chinese language audio guides. BL to investigate costs.

2 Fire risks

JM (Fire officer) warned that fire risks increasing because of unusually dry weather and we are lucky don't to have had any serious incidents. We agreed to put up more warning posters in car parks and at the visitors' centre.

3 Litter

JJ reported back on the anti-litter campaign 'Where's your rubbish' which seems to have been very successful.

4 Meeting attendance

AH said her team had complained about having to attend so many meetings where their presence wasn't strictly necessary. BL agreed to review meeting proceedure.

Date of next meeting: Wendsday 28th September

1 **))) 4.5** **Northern Joy Expeditions is a cruise company. Listen to their promotional audio and mark the statements true (T) or false (F).**

1 The company offers cruises in the Antarctic region.   T/F

2 The cruises begin in Murmansk.   T/F

3 The cruises are probably a high-end product aimed at a wealthy clientele. T/F

4 There are no excursions on foot.   T/F

5 The company markets itself on its environmental credentials.   T/F

2 **Complete the email from the Society for Sustainable Research in the Arctic (SRAR) to the director of Northern Joy with the words in the box.**

degradation   ecosystem   erosion   fauna   harmful   indigenous   species   stress   vegetation

| From: | d.ouspenky@SRARagency.com |
| To: | g.spiller@northernjoy.com |

Dear Sir

As you know, the SRAR is concerned about damage to the area's fragile ¹_____ due to the increased numbers of visitors brought by your cruise ships. All life in these regions, which, as you know, includes many rare ²_____ of flora and ³_____, tends to be highly concentrated on small sites (bird and seal colonies, etc.) and, unfortunately, these sites are the most attractive both for tourists and for nature. Increasing numbers of tourists result in the thin ⁴_____ cover on the tundra being trampled down and, since the ⁵_____ plants are delicate, they take a long time to recover. While the boat excursions to bird colonies located on coastal cliffs are not ⁶_____, the helicopter excursions you propose are dangerous to young birds. Moreover, pursuing polar bears or walruses in motorboats so that tourists can take pictures of them as close as possible can cause them high levels of ⁷_____ . Using inappropriate land transport, such as tractors, causes environmental ⁸_____ if they disturb or destroy the permafrost layer, which results in soil ⁹_____ I would like to invite you to a meeting to discuss these concerns further with myself and my colleague Lev Sergeivich, whom you have already met. Could you let me know a date which would be convenient for you?

Yours faithfully

Denis Ouspenky (Director, SRAR agency)

3 **Read the email again. In what ways do SRAR think that tourist activity might harm or damage:**

a the land   **b** plants   **c** animals?

4 **Match the sentence halves to complete the code of good practice that Northern Joy Expeditions has agreed on with the SRAR.**

1 We will benefit the local economy

2 We will operate in an ecologically responsible manner

3 We will maintain the character of these untouched, remote areas

4 We will respect and involve the local community in our tourism activities

5 We will make it part of our mission to educate visitors about local culture and nature by only employing knowledgeable guides and

a by cooperating in the control of tourist numbers and by supporting local conservation projects.

b and these will not impact the lifestyle of indigenous peoples unless they decide so.

c constantly improving the awareness levels of our personnel.

d by employing staff, buying goods and services, and paying tax locally.

e by establishing and continuously improving environmental policies.

5 COME FLY WITH ME

1

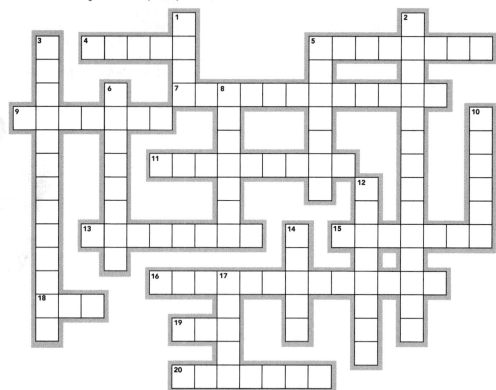

ACROSS

4 Those planes are _____ aircraft. They are designed to carry goods not passengers. (5)

5 Since the events of 9/11, airport _____ has become tighter. (8)

7 The low-cost airline flies to a large number of different _____ in Europe and the Middle East. (12)

9 Passengers are only permitted to take one item of hand _____ on to the plane with them. (7)

11 The airport has excellent _____ , including shops, restaurants and a children's play area. (9)

13 It was a long-haul flight from Sydney to London, with one _____ to refuel. (8)

15 I couldn't find a spare luggage _____ anywhere and was obliged to carry my cases. (7)

16 Bad weather can cause flight _____ since planes cannot take off under certain weather conditions. (13)

18 Your luggage _____ has all of your flight information on it, including your destination. (3)

19 A _____ is an airport which many airlines use as a stopover or transfer point on long-haul flights. (3)

20 Passengers are requested to remain in their seats with their seatbelts fastened during take-off and _____ . (7)

DOWN

1 Bags that do not fit in the overhead lockers will be placed with the other luggage in the _____ . (4)

2 The best airports benefit from fast and cheap _____ _____ to the city centre. (9, 5)

3 Passengers for Paris should proceed to _____ _____ 15 where the aircraft is waiting to depart. (9, 4)

5 A _____ reads the numbers of your luggage bar code. (7)

6 Airports are struggling to increase their _____ to handle ever-growing numbers of passengers. (8)

8 A clear and consistent _____ system is essential to help people find their way around the airport. (7)

10 Air traffic controllers and ground staff must ensure that the _____ is cleared for take-off. (6)

12 An airport _____ is a building where passengers transfer between ground transport and the facilities that allow them to board aircraft. (8)

14 Security alerts are not only very stressful, they can cause a long _____ to your flight. (5)

17 It is the job of the _____ crew to look after passengers during the flight. (5)

2 Complete the text about airport security procedures with the passive form of the verbs in brackets in the appropriate tense and aspect. There may be more than one possible answer.

For the last decade, strict security regulations ¹_____ (enforce) in international airports. Passengers have got used to ²_____ (submit) to time-consuming checks and searches. Shoes ³_____ (must/remove) and all laptops and liquids taken out of passengers' hand luggage and passed through a scanner. In particularly security-conscious states, travellers ⁴_____ (may/ask) to remove their clothes to be thoroughly searched. However, people are beginning to complain that none of the screening procedures that ⁵_____ (implement) until now actually make us feel safer; they just make flying more stressful. In fact, since such procedures ⁶_____ (design) to meet yesterday's threats, they are likely to be unsuccessful in protecting us against the unpredictable threats of the future. The term 'security theatre' ⁷_____ (invent) to describe procedures that make people feel safe by showing that 'something ⁸_____ (do)' even when no measurable increase in security levels ⁹_____ (achieve). What is most worrying is that new airport terminals ¹⁰_____ (design) purely around security, rather than around comfortable and convenient travel. However, security experts assure us that radical changes in airport security ¹¹_____ (plan) and new systems are in development. In the future, the check-in process ¹²_____ (streamline) and waiting times greatly reduced.

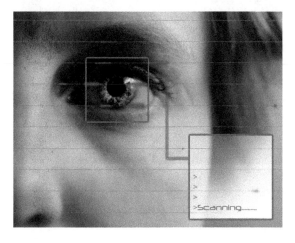

3))) 5.1 Listen to Keith Jackson from the International Air Transport Association discussing the future of airport security. What are the names of the THREE possible routes through security in the 'tunnel system' he describes?

4 Match the sentence beginnings 1–6 with the endings a–f. Then listen again and check.

1 In the old days, an average of 350 people

2 The system we have in place at the moment

3 It will be possible for airline passengers to get their boarding passes

4 The new system we are developing

5 Equipment in each tunnel will scan passengers as they walk through,

6 We're testing these systems now but

a using fingerprint or retinal scans and pass through the security check non-stop.

b we're going to need a bit more time before we can start deploying them.

c meaning no more x-ray machines, emptying pockets or removing shoes and jackets.

d treats every passenger as a potential suspect.

e would normally go through security in an hour.

f will consist of passengers passing through one of three ten-metre-long tunnels.

PRONUNCIATION

5 Put the words in order to make common passenger security questions.

1 pack / these / you / yourself / bags / Did

_____

2 aerosols / Are / gels or / you / carrying / any

_____

3 luggage / objects / any / you / in / Do / your / sharp / have

_____

4 interfered / bags / have / Could / with / your / anyone

_____

5 give / anyone / Did / to / on to / plane / you / anything / carry / the

_____

6))) 5.2 Listen and check your answers. Practise saying the sentences, paying attention to the stress and the way the words are run together.

1 **Choose the best word to complete what flight attendant Davina Del Monte says about dealing with passengers.**

Boarding is probably the most stressful moment of a flight for flight attendants because if there is a **1** *delay / interruption / suspension* or a mechanical problem, then passengers often get **2** *upset / excited / nervous* and shout at us. It's something you get used to and once the first shock of the bad news is over, most passengers **3** *get better / make up / calm down* quite quickly but it's not an easy start to the day. We all have to deal with seriously **4** *assertive / abusive / supportive* passengers at some point but it doesn't happen every day and we are good at supporting each other when there's a serious **5** *happening / incident / event*.

On a day-to-day basis, one of the things I find most **6** *frustrating / fascinating / disappointing* is the way passengers stay plugged into their

electronic **7** *sets / devices / posts*. When I ask a question, no one answers anymore: I feel like I'm talking to myself! It's also increasingly difficult to get people to switch things off during take-off and landing. It's one of the few things I have **8** *words / discussion / rows* with passengers about. Not only can they **9** *hold up / interfere / restrict* with the plane's electronics but if I'm not in my seat for take-off because I'm still dealing with a passenger who won't switch off their iPad, I get **10** *fined / punished / suspended* by the FAA. The money is deducted from my salary at the end of the month and I'm not happy about it! The interesting thing is that (until recently) no electronics in flight has always been the rule. It's never been the rule that's a problem, just some passengers' attitude towards it.

2 **Circle the odd one out in each group.**

1 argument / dispute / settlement / disagreement / row

2 abusive / insulting / offensive / rude / respectful

3 disturbance / inconvenience / incident / nuisance

4 fired / sacked / reinstated / suspended / let go

5 blacklisted / banned / licensed / thrown out

6 frustrated / annoyed / offensive / upset / irritated

3 **Complete the announcements for breaking bad news with the words in the box.**

advised   available   cancellation   delayed
fastened   inconvenience   informed   regret
return   suspended   weather   zone

We would like to inform all passengers to Berlin that, due to the **1**_____ of an earlier flight, there are no more seats **2**_____ until tomorrow morning.

We **7**_____ to inform passengers that Flight 786 to Chicago has been cancelled. We apologize for any **8**_____ caused to our passengers and will keep you **9**_____ of further developments. Please listen for further announcements.

Passengers are **3**_____ that the departure of flight 372 to Munich will be **4**_____ for approximately three-quarters of an hour.

Ladies and gentlemen, we will shortly be passing through a **10**_____ of turbulence. Please **11**_____ to your seats and keep your seat belts **12**_____ . Thank you.

This is an important passenger announcement. Owing to adverse **5**_____ conditions, check-in is currently **6**_____ .

1 Read the text about the proposed expansion of Heathrow airport in London. How might the airport be extended? Who opposes the plan?

Heathrow planning to grow?

The proposal to expand London's Heathrow airport, already a major international hub and one of the largest and busiest airports in the world, has been the subject of fierce debate. Heathrow's facilities were originally designed to accommodate a maximum of 55 million passengers annually but the number of passengers passing through is now approaching nearly 90 million and the airport has been criticised in recent years for its overcrowding and delays. In 2007, a TripAdvisor survey voted Heathrow the world's least favourite airport alongside Chicago's O'Hare airport. The opening of Terminal 5 in 2008 relieved some pressure on terminal facilities; but since Heathrow only has two runways, operating at over 98% of their capacity, there just isn't any room for more flights. Supporters of the scheme to expand by building a third runway and a sixth terminal claim that it is essential to increase the number of routes to emerging markets, with flights to China particularly important. Although the use of larger aircraft such as the Airbus A380 will allow some increase in passenger numbers, it is difficult for airlines to obtain landing slots to enable them to increase their services from the airport. Despite widespread opposition from local residents and environmental groups, it looks as though the plans for Heathrow's third runway may well go ahead.

2 Read the text again and choose true (T) or false (F).

1 The airport can only easily accommodate up to 90 million passengers. T/F

2 Heathrow has had unfavourable reviews on TripAdvisor in recent years. T/F

3 The opening of Terminal 5 has made it easier for airlines to increase their services from the airport. T/F

4 Heathrow already has two runways and five terminals. T/F

5 The pressure on terminal facilities has resulted in problems for Britain's trade relations with China. T/F

6 Using larger aircraft has helped to increase passenger capacity. T/F

3))) 5.3 Listen to an interview with George Vertian, who lives near Heathrow. Apart from environmental concerns and public health issues, what are his TWO main objections to the expansion?

4 Listen again and complete the statements with up to FOUR words.

1 Planning permission for Terminal 5 was secured by guaranteeing that there would be no attempt to _____ .

2 Hundreds of thousands of people are already affected by _____ .

3 The increase in the level of carbon emissions _____ .

4 Air pollution over London is above EU limits, and the government _____ .

5 Heathrow is still Europe's largest hub airport for _____ .

6 Smaller direct flights could be moved, freeing up Heathrow to operate as the _____ .

7 Our research suggests that business travel is actually _____ .

8 Since web technologies make it so easy for people to communicate with each other face-to-face, business people are saving time and money by flying _____ .

6 HERITAGE

1 Look at the information about different world heritage cities and label the texts with the countries in the box. What do you think is the modern name for the city of Tenochtitlan?

Mexico   Nepal   Norway   Tanzania   Turkey

A _____

Kathmandu was isolated from the rest of the world for many centuries **¹**___ in the Himalayas. The city is renowned for its many sculptures, pagodas, temples and palace buildings of exceptional beauty. This remarkable cultural wealth is the **²**___ that evolved during the reign of the Malla kings between the 15th and 18th centuries.

B _____

The ancient city of **Zanzibar** was a major commercial centre in East Africa and was particularly important for the spice trade. The historic city centre, known as 'The Stone Town', has many fine buildings, some of which **³**___ . The city's architecture **⁴**___ of the culture and traditions of the African, Arabic, Indian and European traders who settled there over nearly a millennium.

C _____

Istanbul is one of the most significant cities in history. When it was **⁵**___ , it was called Byzantium. The city was renamed Constantinople in 330 after the Roman emperor Constantine and **⁶**___ – the Roman Empire (330–395), the Byzantine Empire (395–1204 and 1261–1453), the Latin Empire (1204–1261) and the Ottoman Empire (1453–1922).

D _____

The largest Spanish-speaking city in the world was built on an island in Lake Texcoco by the Aztec tribe known as the Mexica. **Tenochtitlan**, as the city was called, **⁷**___ in 1521 by the Spanish, who rebuilt it in accordance with Spanish urban standards. The city today contains many fine examples of colonial Spanish architecture and **⁸**___ , such as the huge Aztec temple, Templo Mayor.

E _____

Most of the urban area of **Bergen** is situated on or close to **⁹**___ overlooking the port, which is still one of the busiest in northern Europe. The old waterfront district of Bryggen retains its medieval harbour character and features the world's **¹⁰**___ of medieval harbour architecture.

2 Read the texts again and match the gaps 1–10 with the phrases a–j below.

a spectacular ice-carved fjords

b founded more than 2,500 years ago

c finest and best-preserved examples

d recently excavated archaeological sites

e is a unique and exotic blend

f date back to the 10th century

g due to its location in a remote valley

h was besieged and finally captured

i served as the capital of four empires

j manifestation of the sophisticated and prosperous society

3))) 6.1 **Listen to an interview with Charles Makamba from Zanzibar talking about the World Heritage selection process. What TWO advantages does he mention of becoming a World Heritage site?**

4 **Listen again and choose the correct answer.**

1 How many countries have ratified the World Heritage treaty?

   a 198   **b** 189   **c** 199

2 How many selection criteria relate to culture and can be used to evaluate a city?

   a ten   **b** four   **c** six

3 Why was Zanzibar selected as a World Heritage city?

   a it's 'a masterpiece of human creative genius'

   b it contains 'superlative natural phenomena'

   c it's 'an outstanding example of a traditional human settlement'

4 How often does the World Heritage committee meet?

   a once every six months   **b** once a year   **c** once every two years

5 Once a city becomes a World Heritage site, who is ultimately responsible for protecting it?

   a the international community   **b** the local people   **c** the government

5 **Rewrite the information about the World Heritage cities using the words in brackets.**

1 At certain times of the year, it was the custom for the Aztecs to carry out human sacrifices to the sun god on the steps of the temple. (would)

2 In the past, Zanzibar was the world's largest producer of cloves. (used to)

3 People say that if the whole world were one country, then Istanbul would be its capital. (it / said)

4 The Vikings may have sailed to America long before Columbus. (it / believed)

5 In the 1960s, Kathmandu was a popular destination for hippy travellers. They usually stayed in an area of the city called Thamel, which is still popular with budget travellers today. (used to / would)

6 Many scholars think that chocolate was discovered by the Aztecs. (it / thought)

6 **Choose the correct option to complete the descriptions of famous buildings.**

1 The Taj Mahal is a *mausoleum / tomb / museum* built by the Emperor Shah Jahan after the death of his beloved wife Mumtaz Mahal, in memory of his love for her.

2 Salisbury cathedral is famous for its 123-metre-high *curve / spire / column*, which is the tallest in the UK.

3 The Parthenon is a Greek *temple / palace / fortified town* dedicated to Athena, the patron goddess of the nearby city of Athens.

4 The roof of the temple is supported by 46 white marble *columns / towers / balustrades*.

5 Many of the towers in the Kremlin in Moscow are topped by large, gilded *domes / balconies / columns*, which have a characteristic round 'onion' shape.

6 The city of Persepolis in northern Iran is the former capital of the Ancient Persian empire. Although no longer inhabited and almost entirely *broken / ruined / discovered*, it is still an incredible place to visit.

1 **Silvana and Tarik are trainee tour guides in Cairo. Read the extracts from their assessments and complete the assessor's notes with the correct form (noun or adjective) of the words in brackets.**

Silvana
Silvana seems to be a natural ¹_____ (perform) and entertained her group with jokes and anecdotes. However, not all of these were relevant to the tour and she doesn't seem to be as ²_____ (know) about the history of the castle as we would wish. Although a warm and ³_____ (welcome) person, Silvana needs to develop more ⁴_____ (sensitive) to her group's individual needs and ⁵_____ (limit). For example, she didn't notice that some of the older people would have appreciated extra ⁶_____ (assist) with the stairs.

Tarik
Tarik's background knowledge of all aspects of the tour was ¹_____ (impress). He had clearly done his ²_____ (search) and had all the facts and figures at his fingertips but he also made the history of the pyramids' construction come ³_____ (life) by telling ⁴_____ (entertain) stories about the pharaohs' lives. However, Tarik seemed to find the physical aspect of the tour ⁵_____ (challenge) and was often visibly out of breath after climbing up steps. He needs to increase his overall level of ⁶_____ (fit) if he wants to succeed in this profession.

2 **Put the words in order to make useful tour-guide phrases.**

1 like to / gardens / me, / If / go out / we'll / follow / you'd / into / the
_____

2 a / stop / for / Why / don't / we / break / here ?
_____

3 I / gallery / retrace / our / suggest / we / steps / to / the
_____

4 we / coach / now / head / back / to / the / Shall ?
_____

5 some / This / for / a / good / you / to / take / is / opportunity / photos
_____

6 way / back / Now / entrance / we'll / the / make / our / to / main
_____

3 **Match the beginnings of the sentences about the history of Cairo 1–6 with the endings a–f.**

1 Cairo was founded in 932 by General Gawhar al-Siqilli, a member

2 A university and an enormous library were built during the reign of the Fatimid dynasty,

3 Throughout the Middle Ages, Cairo flourished as a centre of trade on the spice route

4 In the late Middle Ages, the population fell dramatically due to the Black Death:

5 The city was invaded by Napoleon in 1778

6 During the first half of the 19th century, the viceroys of Egypt modernized Cairo,

a between Europe and Asia.

b of the powerful Fatimid dynasty that dominated the Middle East in the 10th century.

c bringing gas and lighting to the city.

d but was recaptured by the British in 1801.

e establishing Cairo's reputation as a centre of scholarship and learning.

f over 200,000 people were killed by the plague between 1348 and 1517.

1)))**6.2** Listen to a talk about what makes a great museum and complete the five tips below with ONE word in each gap.

Five ways to make a good museum great

1 The museum must have a clear ¹_____ . Whose ²_____ is it telling and, most importantly, who is it telling them to? Knowing your ³_____ is essential.

2 Once you are clear who you're talking to, you need to look for imaginative ways of getting your audience's ⁴_____ . Question your ⁵_____ about the amount of prior cultural ⁶_____ your visitors possess. Think about any short ⁷_____ you can provide.

3 Thirdly, ⁸_____ is more. Don't ⁹_____ your audience with information. Present small themes in layers within one larger topic.

4 Interactive, ¹⁰_____ presentations are no longer an option – they're an ¹¹_____ . You have to find ways to get your visitors to ¹²_____ in the experience your museum offers. Technology isn't the only way to do this but it will be an essential element in your ¹³_____ .

5 Finally, don't forget the ¹⁴_____: good lighting, clear ¹⁵_____ , clean and adequate ¹⁶_____ facilities, a great museum shop and café wherever possible and great marketing.

2 **Choose the correct option to complete the museum exhibit labels.**

1 Roman *earthenware / steel / coal* vase with detail of a woman's head

2 Steam-powered *pipe / pump / jug* used for draining the marshes (mid 19th century)

3 *Fragments / Metal / Cloth* of a Roman pavement, found when excavating the car park area

4 Woman's silver *earring / brooch / necklace*, believed to have been used as cloak fastening

5 Viking warrior's sword and *plate / shield / tool* (late 9th century)

6 Bronze cooking *weapons / utensils / jewellery* found in Viking woman's *grave / burial / museum* to take with her to use in her next life

7 Carved *wooden / pottery / clay* combs and hair ornaments, as worn by a wealthy Anglo-Saxon woman (circa 900)

3 **Put the dates below in chronological order from 1 (oldest) to 10 (most recent).**

☐ the beginning of the 17th century   ☐ the end of the first millennium

☐ 322 years BCE   ☐ the beginning of the 20th century

☐ 500 BCE   ☐ 1984

☐ 1764   ☐ 1661

☐ 2005   ☐ 738 CE

BCE= before common era   CE = common era

PRONUNCIATION

4)))**6.3** Listen and repeat the descriptions of artefacts. Pay attention to the stressed words and syllables in bold and try to run the words together as shown.

1 a **carved jade fig**ure **of a horse**

2 a **flint knife** with an **iv**ory **han**dle

3 a **silver mir**ror **dec**orated with **am**ber

4 an an**tique lea**ther **writ**ing case

5 over **three hun**dred and **fif**ty Chin**ese** ink **pain**tings

6 **frag**ments of a **pain**ted **plas**ter **ceil**ing

7 **Vi**king **cook**ing u**ten**sils

8 an im**mense brown earth**enware **vase**

7 MANAGING EVENTS

UNIT MENU

Grammar: conditional structures
Vocabulary: collocations with events
Professional skills: understanding contracts
Case study: plan a high-profile event

1 **Read the quotes from events organizers. What kind of event does each one refer to? Match the quotes 1-8 with the events in the box.**

> awards ceremony   conference   film première   marathon
> product launch party   rock festival   trade fair   wedding

1 _____

We had to change the venue at the last minute, so some of the exhibitors got a bigger <u>stand</u> than they'd reserved but they didn't complain.

2 _____

Unfortunately, some <u>gatecrashers</u> got in who were only really interested in the food and drink. They cheered when the winners were announced but talked all the way through the acceptance speeches.

3 _____

The florists say they didn't get the message about not using lilies, so unfortunately the bouquets all had lilies in, which the groom was allergic to.

4 _____

Well, there was a last-minute panic because the <u>goodie bags</u> got sent to the wrong place, so the guests nearly went away without any product samples.

5 _____

We must allow at least half an hour for the stars to pose for the <u>photo call</u> on the red carpet, so the actual screening shouldn't start until at least eight o'clock.

6 _____

The speakers all appreciated the on-site technical support as they were setting up. When one of the overhead projectors broke, we managed to replace it within ten minutes.

7 _____

Some people got injured in a front-of-stage <u>crush</u> in the pyramid stage area and the speakers for the sound system were damaged. Fortunately, nobody was badly hurt.

8 _____

We want to be able to offer the kind of prize money that will attract top athletes, so we need to get some more <u>sponsorship</u> from somewhere.

2 **Match the underlined words in the quotes in Exercise 1 with the definitions.**

1 _____ when a big crowd of people are pressed together too closely
2 _____ when the media are invited take pictures of the cast of a film or play
3 _____ a set of items given away at trade shows and conferences as part of a promotion campaign
4 _____ when a business pays some of the costs of the event in return for promotion of its goods and services
5 _____ an exhibition area at a trade fair often with a counter from which goods can be sold
6 _____ people at a party or other event who haven't been invited or don't have a ticket

3 **The verbs below are all connected with events management. In each group, circle the verb which has a different meaning.**

1 stage	put on	organize	liaise with	set up
2 cancel	abandon	cut	call off	put off
3 postpone	delay	put off	call off	reschedule
4 celebrate	mark	commemorate	observe	set up
5 liaise with	communicate	mediate	attend	coordinate
6 charge	sponsor	fund	subsidize	pay for
7 attend	miss	come to	be present at	show up
8 deal with	manage	anticipate	see to	sort out

4 Assistant Events Manager Anke Lars is about to begin a new project. Choose the best options to complete the email from her boss. What kind of event is it?

From:	Olga@fortunatevents.com
To:	Anke@fortunatevents.com
Subject:	Objectives

Hi Anke

In my absence, the first thing you need to do is sit down with the ¹*participants / stakeholders / delegates* and set some ²*objectives / objects / points*. It is vital that they understand why they want to hold this event and what they want to ³*realize / achieve / succeed* from it, and that they communicate this to you.

You must of course ensure that these objectives are *SMART*: that is, specific, measureable, ⁴*acceptable / attainable / achievable*, realistic and time-bound. Once established, these objectives provide direction for everything and the clients will be able to test their return on ⁵*payment / investment / fee* at the end of the event.

Some objectives are easier to measure than others. With a sales conference, the client's objective might be to achieve a certain percentage of ⁶*growth / advance / evolution* in sales or orders, so it's easy to put a number to it. With this upcoming event, it's more difficult since the client doesn't ⁷*stand / want / think* to gain in the same way. But in this kind of general professional conference where the aim is to share knowledge and increase expertise, specific questions on a ⁸*feedback / payback / look back* form could help you measure to what extent this has been successfully accomplished. I can give you some examples if you come by my office later.

Olga

5))) 7.1 Listen to Olga and Anke's discussion after the event. What were the main problems with:

a the building **b** the clients' expectations **c** the catering?

6 Complete the information about how things could have gone better at the event using the phrases below to form conditional structures. Listen again if necessary to help you.

> avoid lots of problems   check it   company provide a free lunch   have time
> not take so long to serve lunch   provide a shuttle bus to the city centre   the food be cheaper
> the layout of the building not be so complicated

1 If the clients had had more realistic expectations of the costs, they _____ .

2 If they hadn't been trying to save money, they _____ .

3 People wouldn't have got lost all the time if _____ .

4 Anke's team would have put up more signs if _____ .

5 They might have noticed that the map was upside down if _____ .

6 If the canteen had been bigger, it _____ .

7 Some delegates might not have complained if _____ .

8 It would have created a lot of goodwill if _____ .

PRONUNCIATION

7))) 7.2 Look at the sentences and think about whether *have* and *had* are likely to be stressed (hæv/hæd) or unstressed (həv/həd). Then listen and underline *have/had* when they are stressed. Listen again, check and repeat.

1 He wouldn't have done it if he had known better.

2 How long have you had this problem?

3 They haven't finished, have they?

4 If they had arrived earlier, we would have started by now.

5 I don't think they had ever discussed it, had they?

1 **Complete the gaps in the contract with phrases a–g. There is one phrase that you do not need.**

a which consent shall not be unreasonably withheld

b within the jurisdiction of

c (hereinafter referred to as 'the Event Planner')

d but for no other purpose without the prior written consent of the Company

e in conformity with the legislation in force

f from (15/09) to (17/09) for a maximum of (900) people

g if the performance thereof is prevented

THIS EVENT PLANNER AGREEMENT is entered into on 12 March 2013
BETWEEN: Klein and Stolz, a division of Alpha Pharmaceuticals, whose registered office is at Schiller Strasse, Stuttgart, Germany (hereinafter referred to as 'the Company')
AND: Action Events, a private limited company whose registered office is at Farwell Place, London, UK [1]___

WHEREAS the Company seeks to hire the Event Planner, this Event Planner Agreement sets forth the relationship between the Parties and their respective rights, duties and obligations, it is hereby agreed as follows:

1 The Company authorizes the Event Planner to organize a conference for medical professionals [2]___ and to provide for this conference all the services described hereunder in Appendix A, attached.

2 Under the terms and conditions of this Agreement, neither party shall have the right to transfer any of its rights or obligations to any other company, firm or person without first obtaining the consent and approval in writing of the other party, [3]___ . Any breach of this term shall render the contract forthwith null and void.

3 Both parties shall keep all commercial and technical information in whatever form acquired in strict confidence and use its best endeavours to bind its employees and agents to do the same.

4 The Event Planner hereby accepts and agrees to use the Company's name and logo in any material used by the Event Planner for the marketing and promotion of the Event [4]___ . Such uses include but are not limited to internet and social media references, television and radio announcements, promotional material in newspapers, magazines or billboards.

5 Neither party shall be considered in default in the performance of its obligations or be responsible for any failure or delay in the execution of such obligations [5]___ or delayed wholly or in part as a consequence, whether direct or indirect, of any cause beyond the reasonable control of and without the fault or negligence of such party.

6 This Agreement shall be governed by and construed in accordance with English law and the parties irrevocably accept and agree that any action based upon any claim of breach arising out of or in connection with this Agreement will be subject to and [6]___ the English courts.

---

2 **Read the completed contract. What kind of event does it relate to and what are the names and the locations of the companies concerned?**

3 **Which of the six sections relates to:**

a subcontracting?

b the legal system under which the contract was drawn up?

c things that could stop either company from fulfilling its responsibilities?

d the circumstances in which the companies' branding can be used?

e the need for both companies to be careful about confidential information relating to the other one?

f the details of the event?

1 )) **7.3** Listen to Anke and Olga discuss a new contract. What kind of event is it and where will it take place? How much is the budget?

2 Choose the best answer for each question. Then listen again to check.

1 The couple are:

a film stars   **b** sports people   **c** celebrities

2 Olga wishes that the event:

a had a bigger budget

b wasn't going to happen so soon

c was in America

3 Anke thinks they will need a special task force to deal with:

a flights   **b** geography   **c** Geeta

4 There will be:

a 250 guests   **b** 215 guests   **c** 260 guests

5 Anke's overall responsibility is for:

a the wedding ceremony

b the reception

c hiring dancers and entertainers

6 Olga thinks they need to have a contingency plan in case:

a they can't get find enough local elephants

b they can't source elephants from other areas of the country

c the locals don't want them to use elephants

7 Taylor has made the planning process more difficult because:

a she wants to increase the budget

b she changes her mind all the time

c she wants fire-eaters for the entertainment for the reception

8 If they include fire-eaters in the entertainment, Anke is worried that:

a the reception can't take place outside

b they can't use marquees with wooden floors

c their insurance premiums will increase

3 The event is now only a month away and things are still not going smoothly. Read Raj's list of problems and match the sentence beginnings 1–6 with the endings a–f.

1 The celebrity guests want to bring their own security

2 The Bollywood dancers have found out what rates we are paying for the foreign musicians

3 The marquee hire company is worried about fire risks

4 The local police say we need to obtain a special licence

5 I have just inspected the toilet facilities at the palace and

6 The caterers have threatened to cancel the contract and enforce the penalty clause

a they are inadequate for the number of guests.

b but we won't have enough accommodation for all the extra staff.

c if we change the menu for the banquet yet again.

d for hiring more than four elephants. This usually takes eight weeks to come through.

e and are demanding a higher fee.

f and is threatening to withdraw from the contract unless we double our deposit.

4 Complete Olga's suggestions with the verbs in the box and match them with the problems.

> agree   arrange   cover   forward
> give   hire   raise

1 _____ the guests responsibility for finding accommodation for their security staff.

2 _____ the dancers' fee to match the rates we are paying the musicians.

3 _____ to pay the increased deposit. The insurance will _____ the costs if anything happens.

4 Find someone who has the elephant licence and _____ for the contract to be in his name.

5 _____ luxury portable toilets from www.fabuloo.com. We'll ship them over.

6 _____ the correspondence about the catering to Taylor. It's her decision.

8 CAREERS

UNIT MENU

Grammar: dependent prepositions
Vocabulary: remuneration; adjectives describing personality
Professional skills: interviews
Case study: recruit the right person

1 **Read the text about extreme job search methods. Fill in the gaps with sentences a–f. There is one sentence you do not need.**

   a However, in order to even get to this point, today's job seekers are using ever more extreme ways of grabbing employers' attention.

   b Of course, there are risks attached because some employers undoubtedly exploit internships as a way of getting free manpower.

   c Doing something to get you noticed can help as much as a good job application.

   d An obvious way to start is by sending out speculative applications to companies you're interested in.

   e You aren't the only one.

   f People need to understand that it's not enough just to get noticed.

Extreme job search

So you're looking for a job? ¹_____ And, as all of you are realizing, in today's increasingly competitive job market, job seekers have to be more proactive to get themselves noticed by prospective employers. ²_____ 'Don't be afraid to make the first move,' says recruitment expert, Yordanka Emil. 'Identify businesses you would like to work for, research how you can contribute to their success and contact them directly.' She also suggests that proposing working for free for a set number of hours each week over several months is an excellent way of getting your foot in the door. ³_____ On the plus side, this strategy affords you an opportunity to demonstrate what the company could gain from hiring you and, in effect, to create a job for yourself. According to Yordanka, once you are 'in', there's at least a 50%

chance this could lead to full-time employment. ⁴_____ Rather than simply sending a CV, job seekers now send videos, presentations and links to websites with photos, slideshows and testimonials. They buy ad space on Facebook or Google, post their resumé on billboards and send cookies and mugs with invitations to coffee to their targeted employers. Sometimes such tactics pay off, but Yordanka, who has several times received a resumé stuffed into a shoe with the note 'just trying to get my foot in the door' and the occasional pizza box that includes the words 'delivering you a great candidate', sounds a note of caution. ⁵_____ A job application has to have some substance. 'It can be interesting with a little personality to it,' she says, 'but gimmicks on their own will not get you hired.'

2 **Match the underlined words in Exercise 1 with the definitions.**

   1 _____ deliver a good result or profit

   2 _____ a trick, scheme or strategy designed to attract attention

   3 _____ when you send your CV and a covering letter to a company in case they have any vacancies in the future

   4 _____ formal written statement to thank or praise a person, or show admiration for what they have done

   5 _____ doing things to create or control a situation rather than just responding to it after it has happened

3)))8.1 **Alison, a hotel manager, and Yusef, a sales executive, are discussing the pay and conditions in their jobs. Complete the conversation with the words and phrases in the box. Then listen and check your answers.**

> commissions   company car   discount   fringe benefits   healthcare   pension
> performance-related pay   retirement   stock options   subsidized

Alison: My pay is OK, about average for the job but I'm certainly not earning big bucks like you do!

Yusef: Actually, my basic annual salary isn't great but in a good year, I can easily double it in sales ¹_____ . I don't think that's going to be case this year, though, as we've just lost a big customer: another chain has offered them conditions we can't possibly match. That's the problem with ²_____ . Your work is measured by results, not by the effort you've put in!

Alison: Does your company offer you any ³_____ , like private ⁴_____ or incentive travel or anything?

Yusef: Not really, unless you count the ⁵_____ . But since driving is so much part of the job, I don't really think of it in those terms. However, the company's ⁶_____ savings scheme is very good. If I stayed in this job for the next 30 years, I'd get an excellent ⁷_____ at the end of it. I can't imagine doing that, though!

Alison: Well, I can stay at any other Elliott Hotel in the world for at least a 50% ⁸_____ and I get ⁹_____ membership of Aqua Leisure Clubs because they're in the same group. When I was made a junior manager, I was offered ¹⁰_____ as well, which is great. And it's clever of the hotel, too because now I feel I've got even more of an interest in making sure the business is a success.

4 **Alison's hotel has advertised a vacancy for the post of head housekeeper. Read the extract from her application. Find and correct EIGHT mistakes to do with dependent prepositions.**

I am writing to apply to the position of housekeeper advertised on your website. Please find attached my CV with details of my qualifications and experience. As you will see, I have over five years' experience at hotel housekeeping, including three as assistant housekeeper at the Yorick Hotel in Stockholm where I now work. I am familiar in all aspects of housekeeping operations, including managing and training teams of cleaning staff. I am currently jointly responsible of a team of 20 full- and part-time chambermaids and maintenance personnel. As well as a detailed knowledge in all aspects of hotel cleaning, I take pride at my excellent organizational skills and attention of detail. I have always been conscious in the extent to which a strong housekeeping team contributes to excellent customer service and have twice won the Yorick Hotel employees' award for exceptional customer service.

1 **Read the text about preparing for job interviews. Choose the best option, a, b or c, for each gap.**

Mistakes to avoid when preparing for interview

A common mistake many candidates make is not doing enough background research into the company into which they hope to be recruited. Having some background knowledge of the ¹___ of the organization and how it operates will not only make you feel better prepared and more ²___ , but it will also help you answer the interviewer's questions in more detail because you have more information to draw on. Furthermore, if it's obvious that you haven't researched the company website and the other applicants have, you can kiss goodbye to your hopes of being ³___ .

It is equally important to be well-prepared as far as talking about yourself is concerned. In fact, there is simply no excuse not to be! ⁴___ and sounding uncertain when trying to answer standard job interview questions such as 'What do you consider your biggest ⁵___ ?' or 'Where do you see yourself in five years?' creates a bad ⁶___ . Of course, you will need to ⁷___ your answers to fit the circumstances each time but you should be clear which skills and strengths you want to ⁸___ in order to demonstrate that you are the best candidate for the job. If you aren't clear what your selling points are, how can you get them across to the interviewer?

1 a formation	**b** structure	**c** make-up
2 a confident	**b** sure	**c** certain
3 a chosen	**b** taken	**c** selected
4 a Waiting	**b** Hesitating	**c** Pausing
5 a lack	**b** problem	**c** weakness
6 a feeling	**b** idea	**c** impression
7 a model	**b** tailor	**c** change
8 a highlight	**b** exaggerate	**c** emphasis

2 **Put the words in order to make six common questions that you could ask or be asked at a job interview.**

1 me / problem / handled / example / you / Can / it / how / you / an / a / of / and / give

2 me / about / involves / something / the / you / more / what / tell / Could / job

3 attractive / you / this / about / do / position / most / What / find

4 your / briefly / previous / through / Could / experience / run / you

5 who / reviewed / and / my / How / be / that / will / performance / does

6 would / How / friend / you / or / a / describe / colleague

3)))8.2 **Listen to four extracts from Joanna's interview for a job as tour leader with an adventure tourism company. Which four questions from Exercise 2 does she answer?**

a ___   b ___   c ___   d ___

4 **Listen again and choose true (T) or false (F).**

1 Joanna thinks that her interpersonal skills are a strong selling point. T/F

2 She has worked on the reception desk of a Spanish hotel. T/F

3 The clients of the educational tour company she worked for were European. T/F

4 She didn't enjoy working with minors. T/F

5 Joanna feels the job would give her the opportunity to develop her customer service skills. T/F

6 One of Joanna's clients had a panic attack when she missed her flight. T/F

1 Choose the best words to complete the job advertisement. What is the job and where is it located?

Job summary

Smart luxury is at the core of everything that Crystal Springs Resorts does. We offer our guests one-of-a-kind experiences and ¹*exceptional / extraordinary / special* levels of customer service.

Core work activities

As a Banquet Manager based at our California resort in San Francisco, you will be an energetic and ²*useful / versatile / all-round* hotel industry professional capable of performing the following tasks to the highest standards:
• Manage all banquets/events
• ³*Hold / Maintain / Keep* outstanding levels of customer service
• Recruit, train, and ⁴*supervise / watch / survey* the Front Office team

Candidate profile

To successfully fill this role, you should be able to demonstrate the following:
• ⁵*Licence / Permit / Degree* or Diploma in Hotel Management or equivalent
• Passion for delivering outstanding customer service
• Experience in a similar role with a proven ⁶*track / field / experience* record in delivering profit and controlling costs
• Strong leadership skills with a ⁷*hands-on / hands-out / hands-forward* approach to people management and team building
• Ability to work in a ⁸*pressure / pressurized / pressured* environment
• Fluent English and, if possible, a good working knowledge of Spanish ⁹*fee / money / remuneration* and benefits
Your benefits will include a competitive starting salary and holiday ¹⁰*time / right / entitlement*.

David Bowden

Jennie Chan

Pedro Gomez

2)))8.3 **Listen to the Crystal Springs Human Resources team discussing the first round of interviews. What problem did several of the candidates have? How many are shortlisted for a second interview?**

3 Listen again. Who:

1 speaks several languages?
2 has worked outside the USA?
3 made a good impression due to his/her appearance?
4 hasn't got enough experience for the job?
5 doesn't have a degree?
6 didn't demonstrate good people skills?
7 seems to be very ambitious?
8 has been headhunted?

4 The team interview Jennie Chan again and decide to offer her the job. Complete the email with the words and phrases in the box.

> delighted to   entitlement   fringe benefits
> look forward to   retirement savings

Dear Ms Chan

Following your recent second interview, we are ¹_____ offer you the position of Banquet Manager. As discussed during the interview, your salary will be $40,000 but you also have some ²_____ : reduced hotel room rates in our hotels worldwide, plus discounts on products and services offered by Golden Lotus Worldwide and its partners.

There is also the opt-out option of our ³_____ scheme. Your annual holiday ⁴_____ is 14 days, plus public holidays.

We'd like to take this opportunity to welcome you into The Golden Lotus family and we ⁵_____ working with you.

Best regards

The Crystal Springs Management Team

PRONUNCIATION

5)))8.4 **Sometimes the stress pattern changes in a word according to what part of speech it is. Say these sentences aloud, paying attention to the underlined words. Then listen and check your answers.**

1 We need to <u>advertise</u> this job. Let's put an <u>advertisement</u> on Google.
2 I'm going to <u>refer</u> to the people who you said would give you <u>references</u>.
3 I got a pay <u>increase</u> last year but I don' think they're going to <u>increase</u> it again soon!
4 If the economy <u>contracts</u> any more, I'll never get a full-time <u>contract</u>.
5 It's an <u>export</u> company but I don't know exactly what they <u>export</u>.

9 GASTRONOMY

UNIT MENU

Grammar: relative clauses

Vocabulary: food and cooking

Professional skills: running a restaurant

Case study: evaluate a restaurant review

1 **Read the texts about different world cuisines. Match the phrases a–f with the gaps 1–5. There is one extra phrase which you do not need.**

a to make the curries for which our cuisine is famous

b presentation is very important in our national cuisine

c a kind of flat bread, which has become popular throughout the world

d many dishes only having between four and eight ingredients

e a mouth-watering, creamy sauce delicately flavoured with garlic

f has a lot of smoked, pickled and salted food in it

2 **Match the countries with the descriptions of their cuisine A–E.**

India Italy Japan Mexico Russia

A _____

Our cuisine ¹_____ because during our long, cold winters, it's difficult to grow fresh <u>produce</u>. We love to combine the sharp flavours of <u>pickled</u> and salted food with <u>bland</u>er tastes, such as <u>grains</u>, especially buckwheat and dairy products. Our cuisine is famous for its delicious soups, such as *shchi*, made out of cabbage and *borscht*, a rich beetroot soup.

B _____

Traditionally, most people have a vegetarian diet for both religious and economic reasons. We eat a lot of rice and use different kinds of spices and <u>aromatic</u> plants ²_____ . In the north, dishes are often based on tomatoes and garlic whereas to the south, coconut milk and citrus fruits are common ingredients.

C _____

As we are an island nation, it's not surprising that our national cuisine features a lot of seafood, often eaten raw and also seaweed. Like many Asian nations, we like rice and noodles and we use <u>piquant</u>, <u>fermented</u> sauces, such as soy sauce, to flavour our food. We think a dish should be a feast for the eyes as well as the stomach, so ³_____ .

D _____

Our modern cuisine is a fusion of traditional native central American cooking and European, especially Spanish, influences. The <u>staple</u> items are corn, beans and chilli peppers, which we eat with different sauces, like *salsa*, a tomato-based sauce and *mole*, a rich, spicy sauce. Most meals are accompanied by tortilla, ⁴_____ .

E _____

Our cuisine is characterized by its extreme simplicity, ⁵_____ . We rely on fresh, high-quality ingredients rather than complicated recipes. Fresh vegetables and herbs are essential in our cuisine, with tomatoes, olive oil and herbs like oregano and basil being staple ingredients. There is a lot of regional variation in the cuisine, and each region has its own varieties of pasta.

3 **Match the underlined words in the text with the definitions.**

1 seeds from certain plants	_____	**5** with a nice smell	_____
2 food obtained through farming	_____	**6** preserved in vinegar	_____
3 main, most common	_____	**7** with a strong, sharp taste	_____
4 without a strong taste	_____	**8** changed chemically by bacteria or yeast	_____

4))) **9.1** **Listen to Tomaso Andreoni, manager of a Turin-based tour company, giving a presentation about the company's future plans in culinary tourism. Answer the questions.**

1 Why does Tomaso think culinary tourism is a logical next step for the company?

2 What values is the 'slow food' movement based on?

3 What culinary tourism product does the company already offer?

5 **Listen again and complete the sentences with TWO or THREE words.**

1 The World Tourism Organization classifies culinary tourism as a branch of _____ .

2 If you're preparing new types of food in different ways, the whole experience can feel _____ .

3 Eating and drinking involve all five of _____ .

4 Clients who take culinary vacations tend to be well-educated, _____ .

5 This goes with another social trend, which is the increasing interest in _____ .

6 I see a lot of potential to combine our tours with visits to _____ .

7 I think we should take our existing 'Gastronomic Tuscany' tour as a model but also _____ .

8 We could add a day learning about Renaissance cooking, with a Renaissance-style dinner in the evening to make it _____ .

6 **Fill in the gaps 1–10 in the itinerary for a new culinary tour for Tomaso's brochure with the words in the box.**

> baked   chopped   creamy   grilled   marinated
> steamed   stuffed   tempt   topped   whet

7 **Circle the correct relative pronoun a–e. There is sometimes more than one possible answer.**

Itinerary

After the transfer from Napoli airport, check in at the stunning four-star Hotel Villa Gabrisa, [a]*that / which / who* is the only hotel in the region with its own gourmet restaurant. We meet for drinks on the terrace overlooking the medieval walled village of Santa Lucia at 7.00 p.m. to [1]_____ our appetites before our first dinner together at the Michelin-starred Villa Gabrisa restaurant.

Monday

This morning's chef is the excellent Flavio Innocenti, [b]*that / which / who* was recently featured in a *New York Times* article. Flavio will teach us to prepare the regional speciality of roast vegetables [2]_____ overnight in truffle oil and white ravioli [3]_____ with farm-fresh ricotta and finely [4]_____ mushrooms. After lunch, we'll visit the historic medieval hill-top village of Monferrato and drop in on some of the local artisans. Tonight's dinner will be at the Osteria Sorrento, where Flavio's team will [5]_____ your palate with a special seven-course degustazióne dinner [c]*that / which / who* has been created to showcase the best regional produce.

Tuesday

Join us for freshly-[6]_____ croissants and cappuccino in the village of Santa Lucia before this morning's cooking class. Luisa di Gregorio, [d]*that / which / who* is our chef this morning, has over 50 years' experience in the kitchen! She will be teaching us to prepare mussels [7]_____ in a large pan with minced garlic, a speciality [e]*that / which / who* is from the Amalfi coast. Our meal will include charcoal-[8]_____ vegetables [9]_____ with local extra virgin olive oil and the most delicious [10]_____, light and fluffy tiramisú you have ever tasted.

GASTRONOMY

1))) 9.2 **Listen to part of a talk by a celebrity chef about how to run a successful restaurant. What does he consider the overall key to success?**

2 Correct the mistakes in the statements below. Listen again and check your answers.

1 Many people spend too much time trying to accumulate enough capital to start their restaurant.

2 It will probably cost between 100,000 and 300,000 dollars to pay for the necessary equipment if you are buying an existing restaurant.

3 It doesn't matter if you underestimate your start-up costs.

4 The second main reason why restaurants fail is by not using local produce.

5 The 'big three' that you need to have when you start a restaurant are a great chef, a great location and great service.

6 If your restaurant isn't located in an area where a lot of people pass through on foot, you are sure to fail.

7 Restaurant managers tend not to put enough effort into setting up good systems.

8 The speaker finds it depressing when a restaurant's level of service is mediocre.

3 Match the beginnings of the tips about giving feedback 1–6 with the endings a–f.

1 Give feedback as soon as possible after something happens:

2 Don't forget about the positive things:

3 Focus on the problem that needs to be solved, not on the person:

4 Create a dialogue by listening attentively to what the other person has to say:

5 Put forward solutions so people can improve in future:

6 Use the feedback sandwich by prefacing negative feedback with praise and ending on a positive note:

a people respond to negative feedback more constructively if it is mixed with praise.

b don't wait for the next scheduled appraisal if you have something important to say.

c the way the conversation ends has the most influence on the way people react to it.

d ask for their views on how to improve the situation.

e treat giving negative feedback as an opportunity to teach people how to do better next time.

f say '**this** needs to improve', not '**you** need to improve'.

4 Read some feedback from a restaurant manager to his staff. Which tip(s) from Exercise 3 does he NOT follow in each case?

1 You are all much, much too slow!

2 The service was very poor at the gala dinner last month. I think we created a bad impression.

3 **A:** I don't understand how the waiting staff made so many mistakes with the orders.

   B: Well, I think that …

   A: And another thing – some people weren't wearing clean aprons.

4 Everything was terrible: the kitchen was in chaos, the communication with the serving staff was non-existent and we ran out of salad.

PRONUNCIATION

5 Put the words in the box into the correct group according to their stress pattern.

> accessible   accumulate   appraisal
> constructively   conversation   disadvantage
> improvement   mediocre   solution

□■□□	□■□□	□□■□

6))) 9.3 **Listen and check your answers. Then listen and repeat.**

1   **Pablo and his son Enrique run a family restaurant. Read the review. What kind of restaurant is it and what is it called?**

> The restaurant was easy to find, thanks to the enormous plastic cactus in the window, of a somewhat unfortunate yellow colour, due, no doubt, to long exposure to the sun. Inside, the ambience is less Mexico, more shopping mall, with fluorescent lighting and loud background music. It feels clean and cheerful but the wipe-down yellow tablecloths, although very functional, seem more suited to a fast-food joint than a down-town restaurant. I was greeted by a charming waiter, swiftly seated, had my order taken and was served with drinks. Encouraged by this and the mouth-watering smells from the kitchen, I waited for my food order to arrive … and waited and waited. I could hear shouting from the kitchen but someone turned up the music to cover the noise. When my food finally arrived, I had a headache, intensified by the increasing heat, due to apparently defective air-conditioning. This was a pity because the refried beans were deliciously spicy, probably the best I've ever tasted and the fresh salsa was excellent. The home-made tortillas, on the other hand, were a disappointment, being tough and dry. The portions were enormous, which always makes me feel uncomfortable. All in all, my experience at the Cactus Cooler left me hot and bothered and I doubt I shall return.

2   **Read the text again. Are the statements true (T) or false (F)? Correct any false statements.**

1   The cactus in the window has been there for a long time.   T/F

2   The reviewer liked the plastic yellow tablecloths.   T/F

3   Initially, the reviewer was impressed by the standard of service.   T/F

4   The food smelled and tasted delicious, especially the tortillas.   T/F

5   The reviewer would have appreciated smaller portions.   T/F

3   ))) 9.4   **Pablo and Enrique are discussing the review. Listen and choose the correct answer.**

1 Pablo:

   a didn't know about these problems before.

   b had forgotten the problems.

   c didn't want to listen to Enrique.

2 Enrique thinks that:

   a this is a good opportunity to make some changes.

   b there isn't any money to make changes.

   c no changes are necessary.

3 Enrique wants to throw away the cactus in the window:

   a to save money.

   b because it looks old-fashioned.

   c to create a cosier ambiance.

4 Enrique suggests that his friend could

   a replace the strip lighting with candles.

   b paint a new sign for the restaurant.

   c work in the kitchen.

5 Granny shouldn't work in the kitchen because her eyesight is bad and she:

   a forgets things.

   b burns the tortilla.

   c adds too much seasoning.

6 The service was slow on the day of the reviewer's visit because Granny had a fight:

   a with Enrique.

   b with the waiter.

   c with the other cook.

10 RISK

UNIT MENU

Grammar: modal verbs
Vocabulary: disasters, risk management
Professional skills: dealing with crises
Case study: assess the *Titanic* disaster

1 **Read what three tourism professionals say about the types of risk they face in their line of work. Match the people with the texts.**

   a head chef   **b** airline executive   **c** hotel manager

2 **Look at the texts again and choose the best word in each case.**

---

1 ___

As with any large property, fire is probably the greatest constant ¹*threat / exposure / warning*, so we take great care with the ²*preservation / maintenance / repair* of all the electrical wiring and heating systems. Another priority is checking the smoke alarms, fire extinguishers and sprinklers in all the key areas of the building, since they limit the ³*destruction / damage / damages* if a fire does break out. It's important to keep the corridors and fire exits free from obstructions at all times so that people can exit the building easily should a fire break out. Other than that, our biggest worry is the security of the building and protecting ourselves and our guests from ⁴*strangers / intruders / incomers* and theft.

2 ___

Not a lot of people outside the industry realize what hazardous places we work in! But if you think about it, they are full of hot surfaces, ⁵*boiling / boiled / cooked* liquids and grease, as well as potentially lethal equipment for food preparation. With many electrical appliances, for example, there is a constant threat of electrocution and water ⁶*spillages / spillings / spills* and grease fires increase the dangers of using electrical appliances. Of course, hygiene is also important and kitchens need to be kept very clean to ⁷*instigate / propagate / mitigate* the risk of food poisoning epidemics. However, this causes its own problems: since everything needs to be washed all the time, many accidents and injuries in our industry are caused by people ⁸*skating / slipping / tripping* on wet floors.

3 ___

In recent years, security risks related to incidences of ⁹*terrorist / terrorism / terror* and hijacking have frequently been associated with our industry. However, such incidents are extremely rare, although of course they always attract a lot of media ¹⁰*cover / exposure / coverage* when they occur. In fact, flying is still one of the safest forms of travel, statistically speaking. Our industry is highly competitive and we are very exposed to currency ¹¹*changings / fluctuations / variation* and price wars, with low-cost airlines trying to undercut larger operators. Rising fuel prices and fuel ¹²*shortages / lacks / cuts* can affect us badly and we are always hit when there is an economic recession. When people have less money, they stop flying.

---

3 **According to the texts in Exercise 2, who, where or what:**

   1 suffers badly at times of economic crisis?

   2 are full of very dangerous equipment

   3 cause a lot of workers in kitchens to fall and injure themselves?

   4 is fire one of the biggest ongoing risks?

   5 increase the dangers of using electrical appliances in kitchens?

   6 are important to keep free from obstructions at all times?

   7 happen very seldom but attract a lot of public attention?

   8 is there a lot competition based on price?

4 **Complete the article about risk management in tourism with the words in the box.**

> channels   ecosystems   eventuality   exposed   hazards
> likelihood   minimize   review   stakeholders   unrest

Natural ¹_____ such as floods, tsunamis and wildfires affect over 200 million people throughout the world every year. Tourism is particularly ²_____ to such events, being reliant both on unpredictable local ³_____ and on the local institutions set up to deal with the disasters they might cause. It isn't possible for tourism companies to foresee every ⁴_____ in all the countries where they operate but all possible efforts must be made to ⁵_____ risk. Essential in the management of risk is establishing clear ⁶_____ of communication between the tourism company, the local authorities and the tourists themselves. This applies at every level of tourism planning, from identifying and analysing possible risks through to treating them. Consulting local ⁷_____ is essential in order to calculate the ⁸_____ of different types of risk, from natural disasters to cases of civil ⁹_____ . Most important of all is the ¹⁰_____ process, whereby the risk management plan is regularly updated with the latest information in order to keep it effective.

5 **))) 10.1** **Listen to the airline executive from Exercise 2 talking about how the low-cost airline Lotta Air failed to manage its risk. Complete the summary with TWO words in each case.**

Lotta Air failed because it couldn't spread the risk of fluctuations in ¹_____ . For its customer service, it relied too much on technology to ²_____ . The company also took a risk on the high performance of its badly under-supported ³_____ and on its staffing policies. Consequently, although its fares were competitive, Lotta Air failed to secure ⁴_____ .

6 **Complete the sentences speculating on Lotta Air's problems with the modal verb in brackets and an appropriate verb from the box.**

> be   be trained   fail   perform   rely   spend   succeed   understand

1 Low-cost airlines are a high-risk business and Lotta Air _____ even if it hadn't made mistakes. (may)

2 Nobody will know for sure, but the airline _____ if fuel prices hadn't risen so steeply. (might)

3 They _____ on technology to replace face-to-face customer service. (should not)

4 Their customers _____ furious when they failed to receive replies to their emails. (must)

5 They _____ enough on web design and maintenance – their website was a mess. (can't)

6 Their ground staff _____ very well because they often didn't seem to know what they were doing. (couldn't)

7 If they had paid them more, their employees _____ better. (might)

8 Lotta Air _____ that the ability to offer excellent customer service is a crucial success factor for an airline. (should)

PRONUNCIATION

7 **))) 10.2** **Listen and write the missing words. Then listen again and repeat, paying particular attention to the weak forms.**

1 They _____ the crash occur.

2 They _____ to escape.

3 People _____ the safety instructions.

4 The ship _____ able to turn in time.

5 They _____ much chance of survival in those temperatures.

6 They _____ an emergency drill as soon as you arrived.

1 Read the email from Bob Greenaway, a risk management consultant in adventure tourism, to Rachel Hanna at Raft Adventure. What two documents does he attach to help her?

From:	Bob@consultancy.com
To:	rachel@Raftad.com
Subject:	Health and Safety review

Dear Rachel

From what you say, it sounds as though it was extremely fortunate that nobody drowned in the incident you described. However, your staff could not have known that the girl in question was likely to have a panic attack. Since you train your staff to screen clients for signs of fear or nervousness and your client answered in the negative to the question about claustrophobia on your health and safety questionnaire, you cannot be held accountable for what happened in the cave.

Judging from the documents you sent me, your health and safety procedures and staff training are all solid, and it is thanks to them that there were no fatalities when the incident occurred. What is important now is how you manage the media coverage of the incident in the immediate future. I attach some guidelines below for this and also a less urgent document about how to put together a company crisis management plan for future reference.

I look forward to discussing these with you on Skype tomorrow.

All best wishes

Bob

2 Read the message again and choose the best answers.

1 The incident happened:

a in a boat

b on a train

c in a cave

2 The client:

a hadn't completed the health and safety questionnaire

b panicked

c got stuck in a cave

3 Rachel's staff:

a didn't know the girl had claustrophobia

b didn't check if the girl looked nervous

c didn't follow health and safety procedure

4 Bob thinks that Rachel's company:

a needs to improve its health and safety procedures

b could have done more to prevent the incident

c is not to blame for the incident

5 The incident resulted in the death of:

a a girl

b a staff member

c no one

6 In the immediate future, Rachel needs advice on how to:

a Skype

b talk to the media

c put together a crisis management plan

3 Look at the extracts from Bob's crisis management plan below. Match the beginnings of the sentences 1–6 with the endings a–f.

1 Anticipate every imaginable situation that might arise,

2 Identify the records to be completed in an emergency

3 When an incident occurs, don't waste time hesitating:

4 Formulate a communications strategy with guidelines

5 Set up a hotline

6 Conduct a post-crisis review to learn the lessons from the incident

a for how to manage the media in the event of a major crisis.

b and how to complete and submit them.

c to keep relatives and friends adequately informed.

d starting with those that are most likely to happen.

e and ensure that it does not happen again.

f act promptly to prevent the situation from escalating.

1)) 10.3 **Listen to an account of a badly-managed crisis. What caused the accident? What was the main reason why so many people died?**

2 **Listen again and correct the information in these sentences.**

1 The ship was unsinkable.

2 Only 15% of the required lifeboats were on board.

3 Many sailors were recruited a week before the ship sank.

4 The Captain never realized the ship was heading towards an iceberg.

5 The helmsman got confused because the communication system had changed.

6 People started jumping into the water when all the lifeboats were full.

7 The gate was ordered to be locked to prevent the third-class passengers escaping.

8 The ship couldn't stop moving after the collision, so it took water on more quickly.

3 **Read the text about the lessons that modern risk-management professionals can learn from the *Titanic*. Match the headings A–F with the paragraphs 1–5. There is one extra heading that you do not need.**

A Little things add up

B Health and safety come first

C Never underestimate the human factor

D Beware of overconfidence

E Assumptions are dangerous

F The risks of technology

Five Lessons Security and Risk Professionals can learn from the *Titanic*

1 ___
People were certain the *Titanic* was unsinkable. However, every project risks its iceberg: things can always go wrong and it is important to plan for the worst-case scenarios.

2 ___
Experts believe the worst mistakes were made by the crew of the *Titanic*. We tend to focus on technology and equipment, forgetting that human disasters always involve people – who are not infallible.

3 ___
The owner of the *Titanic* provided the minimum number of lifeboats to maximize space for the wealthiest passengers. The lifeboat drill didn't take place at the appointed time because it was cancelled due to another event. This led passengers to believe the call to the lifeboats was only a drill – which they could ignore.

4 ___
When a passing ship tried to contact the *Titanic* with a warning message about nearby icebergs, the wireless operator was busy sending messages out for passengers and didn't want to be interrupted. He assumed that the message was just a greeting from a passing vessel.

5 ___
A number of small factors played a role in the *Titanic* disaster, for example, the lookouts on the ship had no binoculars because they had been left behind. All too often, the answer to the question of how a disaster happened is: 'one detail at a time'.

4 **Read the text again. Are the statements true (T) or false (F)?**

1 Planning for the worst is a waste of time   T/F

2 For the owner of the *Titanic,* pleasing his richest passengers was more important than meeting safety regulations   T/F

3 Some passengers didn't get into the lifeboats because they thought it wasn't a real emergency.   T/F

4 The wireless operator didn't believe the warning message about the icebergs.   T/F

5 The ship's lookouts forgot to use their binoculars.   T/F

TOURISM TERMS

People

ADL	Adult
CHD	Child
INF	Infant (up to two years old)
MR	Mister
MISS	Used before a single woman's family name
MRS	Used before a married woman's family name
MS	Used before a woman's family name when she does not want to be called 'Mrs' or 'Miss'
PAX	Passengers
VIP	Very important person
VFR	Visiting Friends and Relatives

International organizations

ATLAS	The Association for Tourism and Leisure Education
ETC	European Travel Commission
EU	European Union
IATA	International Air Transport Association – industry trade group for airlines which regulates international air travel
ICAO	International Civil Aviation Organization
IOC	International Olympic Committee
ISO	International Organization for Standardization
NTO	National Tourism Organization (organization a government uses to promote the country)
TIC	Tourist Information Centre
UN	United Nations
UNESCO	United Nations Educational, Scientific and Cultural Organization
VIC	Visitor Information Centre
WTO	World Tourism Organization (also UNWTO)
WHS	World Heritage Site

Jobs in tourism

ASST	Assistant
CEO	Chief Executive Officer
CFO	Chief Financial Officer
CV	Curriculum vitae
DOB	Date of birth
EHK	Executive Housekeeper
FOM	Front Office Manager
FT	Full-time
GM	General Manager
HK	Housekeeper
HQ	Headquarters
HR	Human Resources
HRS	Hours of work
MOD	Manager on duty
PERM	Permanent position
PT	Part-time
TA	Travel agent
TEMP	Temporary position
P/H	Rate of pay per hour
P/W	Per week
P.A.	Per annum (annual salary)

Times and time zones

a.m.	from midnight to noon
p.m.	after noon

12-hour clock	24-hour clock
12.10 a.m.	0010
03.05 a.m.	0305
07.59 p.m.	1959

The 24-hour clock is simpler than the 12-hour clock. It uses four continuous digits (from 0000 to 2400) and there is no a.m. or p.m.

CST	Central Standard Time
EST	Eastern Standard Time
GMT	Greenwich Mean Time
PST	Pacific Standard Time
UTC	Coordinated Universal Time
WST	Western Standard Time

24/7	24 hours a day, 7 days a week
HRS	Hours
WKS	Weeks

Money and prices

Add-ons	Additional tour features that are not included in tour price
Approx.	Approximately

ATM	Automatic Teller Machine (Am Eng), Cash machine (Br Eng)
B	Billions
EXCL	Exclusive (not everything is included in the price)
FIT	Fully inclusive tour
GDP	Gross Domestic Product
GIT	Group Inclusive Tour
GST	General Sales Tax (Am Eng)
IBAN	International Bank Account Number
IIT	Individual Inclusive Tour
INCL	Inclusive
IT	Inclusive tour
K	Thousands
M	Millions
PIN	Personal Identification Number
POS	Point-of-sales terminal (small hand-held computer for servers to take orders and calculate bills)
PP	Per person
VAT	Value added tax (Br Eng)

ISO Currency codes

*World's top ten most traded currencies

AUD	Australian Dollar*
CAD	Canadian Dollar*
CNY	Chinese Yuan Renminbi
EUR	Euro*
GBP	United Kingdom Pound*
HKD	Hong Kong Dollar*
INR	Indian Rupee
JPY	Japanese Yen*
KRW	South Korean Won
MXN	Mexican Peso
NOK	Norwegian Krone*
PLN	Polish Zloty
RUB	Russian Ruble
SEK	Swedish Krone*
CHF	Swiss Franc*
THB	Thai Baht
TRY	Turkish Lira
USD	United States Dollar*

Hotels

AC	Air conditioning
AI or ALL INCL	All-inclusive (price includes accommodation and all food, drink and activities)
BB	Bed & breakfast (price includes accommodation and breakfast only)
DBL	Double room
DLX	Deluxe room
FB	Full board (price includes accommodation and all meals)
HB	Half board (price includes accommodation, breakfast and evening meal)
HTL	Hotel
NTS	Nights
RO	Room only (price for accommodation only)
SC	Self-catering accommodation
SGL	Single room
STD	Standard room
TRPL	Triple room
TWN	Twin room
TWNB	Twin room with bath
TWNS	Twin room with shower
WC	Toilet
YHA	Youth Hostel Association

ISO Country codes

ISO is the widely used international standard. *The ISO two-letter country codes are used for Internet domains.

Country	ISO 2-letter code*	ISO 3-letter code
Australia	AU	AUS
Austria	AT	AUT
Bhutan	BT	BTN
Canada	CA	CAN
China	CN	CHN
Costa Rica	CR	CRI
France	FR	FRA
Germany	DE	DEU
India	IN	IND
Italy	IT	ITA
Kenya	KE	KEN
Korea, Republic of	KR	KOR
Malaysia	MY	MYS
Mexico	MX	MEX
New Zealand	NZ	NZL
Peru	PE	PER
Poland	PL	POL
Russia	RU	RUS
Spain	ES	ESP
Thailand	TH	THA
Turkey	TR	TUR
United Kingdom	GB	GBR
United States	US	USA

Air travel

ARR	Arrival
ATC	Air traffic control
DEP	Departure
ETA	Estimated time of arrival
ETD	Estimated time of departure
ID	Identification
LCC	Low-cost carrier
OW	One-way
RT	Return (Br Eng), Round trip (Am Eng)
SOP	Standard operating procedure
TRSF	Transfer

World's busiest airports
(by international passenger traffic)

LHR	London Heathrow Airport, UK
DXB	Dubai International Airport, United Arab Emirates
HKG	Hong Kong International Airport, Hong Kong
CDG	Paris Charles de Gaulle Airport, France
SIN	Singapore Changi Airport, Singapore
FRA	Frankfurt Airport, Germany
AMS	Amsterdam Airport Schiphol, Netherlands
BKK	Suvarnabhumi Airport, Thailand
ICN	Incheon International Airport, South Korea
NRT	Narita International Airport, Tokyo, Japan

Most visited cities in the world

PAR	Paris
LON	London
BKK	Bangkok
SIN	Singapore
KUL	Kuala Lumpur
NYC	New York
DXB	Dubai
IST	Istanbul
HKG	Hong Kong
SHA	Shanghai

E-mail and letters

ASAP	As soon as possible
BTW	By the way
FYI	For your information
CC	Carbon copy (when a copy of a letter is sent to more than one person)
ENC.	Enclosure (when other papers are included with a letter)
PS	Postscript (when you want to add something after you've finished and signed it)
RSVP	Please reply

Business/Other terms

4Ps	The marketing mix: product, price, promotion, place
7Ps	The extended marketing mix: product, price, promotion, place, people, processes, physical evidence
LEED	Leadership in Energy & Environmental Design standards
SWOT	Strengths, Weaknesses, Opportunities, Threats analysis

Technology

Apps	Applications
CCTV	Closed circuit television
QR code	Quick response code
WI-FI	Wireless fidelity

Unit 1

1.1

M = Marc , S = Sharon , A = Andrei

1

M My brothers and I used to spend the whole summer at my grandmother's house in the South of France. She would look after us while our parents were working in Paris. There was a whole band of us, with our cousins too, and I have very happy memories of those times – the holidays seemed to last forever. Nowadays, I get very little time off, just a few days, so when I do, I want an intense experience to get my adrenalin going and help me forget the stress of work and my Paris life. I like extreme sports and wild places. In the winter, I go heli-skiing in Canada and last summer I went trekking in the Sahara desert.

2

S Essex isn't known for its warm and sunny weather, so my mum and dad were always chasing the sun when we went on holiday. Our family were classic package holidaymakers. We went to Spain mostly, and sometimes to Greece, always on the cheap with a big group of other Brits. My dad always got sunburned and my mum would only ever eat British food and didn't get on with the foreign stuff. Nowadays, I couldn't face going abroad. We have three kids and it would be too complicated and too expensive. The adults just want to relax and recharge our batteries while the kids need space and things to keep them occupied. We usually rent a chalet or a holiday home somewhere by the sea where there's lots of activities for the kids to do.

3

A As you know, things have changed a lot in Russia over the last 20 years: people of my generation have opportunities to travel that our parents never had. For me, travel is all about culture, and my wife and I are making our way round the capitals of Europe. We are experts in budget travel so we usually go with a group because it's cheaper, but we quite often go off on our own. Seeing Rome was an experience I'll never forget – you walk round the corner and suddenly you're in the middle of these ancient ruins! When I was a child, most ordinary people didn't travel much. I used to get sent on youth camps to Sochi near the Black Sea, which I hated, but I loved staying with my grandparents in Odessa.

1.2

1 sing
2 come in
3 calling
4 bringing
5 ring in
6 looking

1.3

1 seeing – sing
2 coming – come in
3 calling – call in
4 bringing - bring in
5 ringing - ring in
6 looking – look-in

1.4

According to the latest reports from the UK tourism agency Visit Britain, 'grey tourism' is set to increase steadily in the UK as more senior citizens are visiting from abroad. Last year, for example, 5.4 million over 55s came to Britain on holiday from overseas – almost one in five of the total number of visitors. This is a sharp increase from 1993, when the ratio was one in eight.

The largest group of grey tourism visitors is British ex-pats, followed by Americans, but the research also showed that there will be a sharp hike in the number of visits to the UK by people from the fast-growing, so-called BRIC economies of Brazil, Russia, India and China. Visitors from China are likely to increase by 89% over the next four years, bringing almost 100,000 extra travellers to the UK by 2014. Indian tourist numbers are also predicted to rise 29%, with visits from Russians going up 24% and Brazilians' visits rising 18%.

So what are the reasons for the popularity of the UK as a destination for senior travellers? According to Visit Britain, the main reason is simply that the country has a good image with this age group. According to their research, over 55s generally have a more positive perception of Britain than younger people and they rank the UK third on the list of countries they would visit if money were no object. Although not all these projected new visitors will be seniors, tourism providers have a vested interest in tailoring their offers to this growing market segment. Grey travellers are usually financially independent and increasingly adventurous, but they are also hungry for attention and enjoy the personal touch.

Unit 2

2.1

J = Javier, M = Megan

J Basically, we really like it, Megan, especially the bright colours. They could have made it look childish, but they're really cool. The graphics also look great. We were worried that some of them looked a bit ugly in the samples, but they work really well on screen, just as you said they would! There's just one thing: the version of the home page with the sound effects just takes too long to load. I love having the birdsong and the sound of the kayak paddling, but we think that the delay while it's loading is too long, so people could lose interest or think the site isn't working, and obviously we can't risk that.

M Mmm, that's weird. When I load it here, it starts almost immediately. Perhaps there's a problem with the MP3 files in the version I sent you. Let me have a look at it and get back to you. What did you think of the drop-down menus from the main tabs?

J Actually, we've decided that we'd prefer potential clients to be able to see these menu items straight away, without having to mouse over them. For example, on the kayaking tab we'd like the menu of the different sorts of kayaking expeditions to be visible *without* having to click on or mouse over anything, so that it's really obvious how much choice we can offer.

M OK, no problem – it's not difficult to take that feature out. Anything else?

J The only other thing is the fonts. We think generally they're a bit small, especially for people accessing the site from a mobile phone. Could you possibly take everything up a point size? Oh, and wait a minute, Scott's trying to tell me something … Yes, he wants to add a link through to his expedition blog from the home page. Would that be OK?

2.2

audience customers easily negative newsletter targeted amendment correctly enables essential increasing remember

2.3

G = Georgia, M = Morley

G Obviously, we need to start developing a social media presence, and I think that our target market is an advantage here: 14- to 17-year-olds are some of the most prolific social media users around, though of course we'll need to be careful with security issues with minors. I think we should start simply by setting up a Facebook page with our profile and posting stories and news from our different holiday camps and sites. We must make sure people have a reason to log on to our Facebook pages when they get back from their holiday – for news or photos or the results of a competition, or whatever. If we link the Facebook account to our website and vice versa, we should soon find that the traffic to both starts building up.

M Yes, OK, but what content should we post? This is what I still don't understand about the whole social media thing.

G Well, I think we should tell stories, ones that we don't mind sharing, that is, about what goes on behind the scenes on the camps, interesting things that happen and people who have done remarkable things. The whole point about social media is that it's just that, social. If we get people interacting with us socially, posting on our wall, tagging photos, etc., that builds up a sense of community as well as spreading information about what we have to offer.

M And what if we get an unhappy customer for some reason, who posts something bad. I've heard some terrible stories about things that have happened as a result of negative reviews on TripAdvisor.

G Well, at least you'll know what the perceived problem is and can react to it immediately, and this can actually end up having a positive effect. Customers can see you're listening to their concerns and that you care.

Unit 3

3.1

A = Alison, C = Chuck

A So, Chuck, are the 'hotels of the future' really going to be under the sea or orbiting round the moon out in space?

C Well sure, Alison, these kinds of places exist already or will definitely do so very soon. But they are at the high end of the spectrum. We're more interested in what ordinary, mainstream hotels are going to look like. We think that technology is very likely to play a leading role in the evolution of the industry. For example, as hotel systems everywhere become interlinked and automated, fewer people are needed to run them, so the chances are that the hotels of the future will have significantly fewer staff than hotels do now. Receptionists will probably be the first to go since checking in could very soon be a thing of the past: the hotel will know who you are the moment you walk in the door thanks to iris scanning technology or face-recognition systems. Some companies may soon start using robots to clean bedrooms as well.

A That all sounds very impersonal. Do you really think this is going to improve services for customers?

C Well, funnily enough, the likelihood is that your hotel experience will actually become much more personalized rather than the other way round. When you make your reservation, the hotel systems will capture so much data about you they will be able to cater for your every need and preference. Infrared entry sensors will register your presence as soon as you enter your room and will regulate the temperature, lighting and entertainment options. The minibar will order your favourite snacks and beverages and the bathroom your preferred toiletries.

A But isn't it a bit risky to leave everything up to computers? I mean, they are bound to go wrong sometimes. And won't people miss the human contact?

C Well, yes, both those things are true – and small hotels might struggle initially with the cost of installing and maintaining the new technology. Already technically-enabled hotels are finding they need to employ full-time on-site IT professionals to keep their systems operational.

3.2

S = Sally, A = Accountant, M = Michael

S What we're not sure about is how to calculate the room rate.

A How many rooms do you plan to have?

S Four.

A OK. Well, it depends on your rate of occupancy – how many bed nights you can sell. Let's take the worst-case scenario.

You have start-up costs for the first year of 34,100 euros and let's say for the sake of argument that you want a return on your investment of … well, how much do you think in your first year?

S Um, well, according to our calculations, we need to make a minimum of 25,900 euros in the first year to keep it all going.

A OK, well that would give you a target of 60,000 euros worth of bed nights to sell. But if you think you're only going to manage to sell 300 bed nights, you would have to charge 60,000 divided by 300 which is … 200 euros.

M Don't you think that's a bit much?

A Well, that would depend on the quality of the accommodation you have to offer and the competition, wouldn't it? But you know your markets better than I do, and anyway it's only an example. Let's suppose a better scenario where you sold 1,000 bed nights – that's an occupancy rate of about 60%. Then you could charge 60,000 euros divided by 1,000, which equals 60 euros, and that probably makes you very competitive. But perhaps you don't want to position yourselves in that price bracket …

3.3

LJ = Lu Jin, N = Naomi

LJ So Naomi, have you and your partners thought of investing in a hotel franchise? The Golden Dragon Country Club Hotel is looking for franchise partners in Guangzhou and they're interested in the same kind of locations outside the city as you are.

N Well, we hadn't seriously considered it up to now, but actually, our concept would fit quite well within the profile of the Golden Dragon Country Club. I know their Shanghai and Macau hotels very well – I love them. But, I don't know … it would be a big change of plan. What would be the main benefits in your view?

LJ Well, for you as the franchisee, the main benefit lies in the reputation of the brand name, and the instant recognition it gives you in the market. You would also have access to Golden Dragon's global distribution systems and customer loyalty programmes to kick-start your marketing, not to mention training programmes and operational know-how that have helped to make the franchise so successful up to now.

N Yes, but we'd still have the same start-up expenses, plus an up-front franchise fee as well as ongoing royalties wouldn't we?

LJ True, but you'd benefit from a much smoother and more rapid start-up riding on the back of all that acquired expertise and you'd have an instant global profile without any initial promotional spend. It's the assistance prior to launch, the staff training and the quality control that would be so helpful to you. But it would also mean you'd have to comply with all the brand's policies, so you'd have to make sure you would be happy about that. Listen, I can put you in touch with Michael Yu, the South-East China franchise manager. Why don't you have a meeting and talk about it?

3.4

1	16,000	600,000	60,000
2	1.4	40,000	14,000
3	12,000,000	120,000	12,000
4	700,000	70,000	17,000
5	9.19	19,000	90,000
6	88,000	80,000	18,000

Unit 4

4.1

I believe that certain changes need to be made to Dubai's tourism industry in order for it to be more sustainable. First of all, Dubai was quite badly hit by the economic crisis of 2008–2009 and we need to be aware that Dubai can't offer much in the way of historic or cultural attractions, as, for example, our neighbours in Oman or Qatar can, so we need to find a way of compensating for that. Dubai is all about shopping and man-made entertainment: we have excellent, world-class amenities, but we need to leverage them to target a wider range of consumers. For example, we could repurpose some of our existing hotels to focus on family tourism and to boost occupancy. For the next stage in our tourism development strategy, we will be investing billions of dollars in a new family-focused entertainment complex to be called Dubailand. We see potential for developing accommodation and entertainment packages like those that Disney World in Florida or Disneyland Paris offer, and have proposed creating transport connections between Dubailand and certain nearby hotels. Most importantly of all, we believe that Dubai's tourism industry needs more private-sector stakeholders. State and government bodies have too much power. Private-sector stakeholders would adopt an investment policy that would be uniquely guided by profit-seeking motives, rather than issues of prestige or local status. For example, we need to be prepared to offer more budget hotels. The main reason why Dubai was so badly hit by the economic recession was that there were no alternatives to four- or five-star accommodation, and so tourists simply went elsewhere.

4.2

D = Doris, L = Leroy, C = Carlton

D OK, I admit that there are jobs now, but what kind of jobs? It's OK if you want to earn local wages as a bartender, but at management level, foreigners outnumber locals by ten to one at least – that's not fair! All the real profit leaks away back to the multinational providers.

L What worries me most is the environmental damage, especially to the coral reefs, caused by water pollution. Some of the hotels have problems with sewage disposal and they illegally dump it in the sea.

C No, that's simply not true anymore, Leroy! Have you forgotten about all the new regulations in place to protect local plants and wildlife? Most hotels now have recycling programmes to help manage their waste. As for getting a better job, Doris, why don't you try and improve your qualifications like I did?

L But, come on, Carlton, look at what's happened to local property prices – a house on the waterfront can sell for a million dollars now. It's not surprising that crime rates and violence have risen in the downtown tourist area, and it's going to get worse, you mark my words. Tension is growing between the police and the street gangs.

C OK, it's true that development brings its own problems, but you can't stop progress!

4.3

1 leak reach sit meet
2 mark arm plant brand
3 short sport hot warn
4 each reef still mean
5 palm part back dark
6 more what bought salt
7 gang range state stage
8 food book new too

4.4

S = Solomon, A = Anja

S So what decisions were made about the visitors' centre in yesterday's meeting, then?

A Decisions, you've got to be joking! We discussed everything we talked about at the last meeting all over again but, as far as I recall – and we haven't had any minutes yet – we hardly decided a single thing.

S Oh. Was it a long meeting?

A Don't ask! It started at 11.00 so it broke up the morning and we went on until after one, by which point everyone was starving, so we stopped for lunch, but we'd only covered half the agenda so we had to reconvene at 1.30. Then Jeremy – and a few other people who aren't worried about wasting everyone else's time – didn't show up until after 2.00, so by the time we finished it was nearly 4.00 and I'd lost nearly a day's work.

S Who's Jeremy?

A Didn't you know? He's the new Digital Communications Manager. He's quite nice really, but he's always late for everything and he never stops talking. Barnaby let him go on and on.

S I'm surprised he got a word in edgeways – it's usually Barnaby who dominates everything!

A Yes, I suppose that makes a change – but Barnaby really is a truly terrible chair. He lets the people with the loudest voices monopolize everything. It feels like there's no one in charge. With no one to control the discussion, we often digress and go right off the agenda, so everything takes ages. Besides which, half of us didn't really know why we were there. If it was a meeting about the visitors' centre, why were we talking about digital promotions most of the time? And if Jeremy and

Barnaby really want to discuss digital promotion, that's fine, but do we all have to be there? Does the whole department have to waste half a day just sitting there listening to them when we've got more than enough to do? You know, I …

4.5

Northern Joy Expeditions is a Polar cruise company offering nature-based cruises to remote destinations in the Arctic. Our small-ship expedition cruises are all about exceptional customer service and environmental values. Sailing from St Petersburg via Murmansk in luxury and comfort as our special guest, you have the exceptional opportunity to witness the beauty of such remote regions as Franz-Josef-Land Archipelago and the Wrangel Islands, which support a wide range of rare bird species and wildlife. You will sail past towering, majestic icebergs, explore the ice floe edge by Zodiac, walk on the tundra and spot unique wildlife such as walruses, whales and polar bears. With our limited passenger numbers and our commitment to ecological conservation, we consider ourselves the new pioneers of polar expedition cruising.

Unit 5

5.1

Well, in the old days, an average of 350 people would normally go through security in an hour, but now the number is down to about 150 in an hour, but we are hoping to change all that. The system we have in place at the moment, in effect, treats every passenger as a potential suspect, that is a potential terrorist, with no regard to how realistic that might be. We've realized that we need to develop a more sophisticated approach. Our goal is that within the next ten years, it will be possible for airline passengers to get their boarding passes using fingerprint or retinal scans and pass through the security check non-stop.

Basically, the new system we are developing will consist of passengers passing through one of three ten-metre-long tunnels. One tunnel will be for 'known travellers', passengers who fly this route frequently and/or have submitted personal data in advance of their trip. The second will be for 'standard' passengers. And the third, the 'enhanced' tunnel, will be for anyone that the security personnel feel needs extra scrutiny. Equipment in each tunnel will scan passengers as they walk through, meaning no more x-ray machines, emptying pockets or removing shoes and jackets. We're testing these systems now but we're going to need a bit more time before we can start deploying them. We have to be sure that they're going to work every time, no matter what, even if, for example, a bottle of water gets spilled down them or there's a power problem.

5.2

1 Did you pack these bags yourself?
2 Are you carrying any gels or aerosols?
3 Do you have any sharp objects in your luggage?
4 Could anyone have interfered with your bags?
5 Did anyone give you anything to carry on to the plane?

5.3

J = Journalist, G = George

J So, is your objection to the construction of the new runway mainly related to how it would affect the environment and the quality of life for people in this area of London?

G There are many reasons why I'm opposed to this project, but that's a good place to start. Planning permission for Terminal 5 was only secured by guaranteeing local residents that there would be no attempt to build a third runway. We're extremely disappointed by the government and the British Aviation Authority's failure to keep their promises in this respect. Hundreds of thousands of people are already affected by noise pollution from Heathrow, and the third runway would dramatically increase the number of people living in the impact area. Thousands of people would have to be relocated and a whole village, the village of Sipton, would be destroyed. The increase in the level of carbon emissions would be catastrophic. Air pollution over London is above EU limits as it is, meaning the city is not meeting its agreements and the government could be fined. And that is quite apart from all the permanent damage to the local ecosystem and the health of local inhabitants.

J It's true that it's difficult to defend airport growth in environmental terms, but what about the long-term economic benefits in terms of job creation and economic growth, as well as maintaining Heathrow's position as a leading global hub?

G Heathrow is still Europe's largest hub airport for connections to emerging economies, so it is not as if we lack these connections – the fear is simply that we may not be number one by 2016. While Heathrow is full, there is spare capacity at Stansted and Gatwick. Smaller direct flights could be moved there, freeing up Heathrow to operate as the hub for international flights. Besides which, while the government has made general statements about the supposed benefits of increased air capacity for 'business', it remains vague about what these actually consist of. Our research suggests that business travel is actually falling rather than increasing. Since web technologies make it so easy for people to communicate with each other face-to-face in real time, business people are actually saving time and money by flying less not more.

Unit 6

6.1

I = Interviewer, C = Charles

I So, Charles, how do you get your city listed as a World Heritage site – and what are the benefits if you do?

C Well, first of all, a place can *only* be nominated by the national government of a country that has signed and ratified the World Heritage Convention and then only if it meets at least one of the official selection criteria set by UNESCO.

I Oh, OK. So how do you know if your country has signed the treaty or not?

C Well, most countries in the world have signed the treaty. As of this year, 189 states have signed it since it was first adopted by the United Nations in 1972, so it's pretty universal.

I I see. And could you tell us a bit more about these selection criteria?

C There are ten selection criteria for World Heritage sites, but six of them relate to culture and four of them to the natural world, so your site will probably be in one category or the other, but not both. For example, a possible criterion for nominating a site on cultural grounds could be that it represents 'a masterpiece of human creative genius'. This would be fine to nominate a building, but wouldn't do for a national park. To nominate a natural site, you would look at criteria such as whether it contains 'superlative natural phenomena or areas of exceptional natural beauty and aesthetic importance'.

I And what about a city?

C Well, for example, we submitted the nomination for The Stone Town in Zanzibar City on the grounds that it was 'an outstanding example of a traditional human settlement'.

I And your nomination was successful.

C Yes. When the selection committee had its annual meeting to consider new nominations, they decided to include our city on the list – I'm delighted to say.

I And once a place is a World Heritage site, what difference does that make? Do you get access to any funding for conservation or restoration projects?

C Well, there is some funding available, but as you can imagine, there is lots of competition for it! The advantage of having your city listed as a World Heritage site is firstly, the recognition in the eyes of the world that it has something exceptional to offer; this is obviously good for developing tourism and the local economy. Secondly, it affords some degree of protection against the site being sold or destroyed, or 'developed' in inappropriate ways. But ultimately, the responsibility still rests with the locals. We have support and guidance from the international community, but it is up to us to protect and preserve our precious heritage.

6.2

What's the secret of a good museum? I'm going to begin by quickly summarizing the top five characteristics which distinguish a good museum from a merely adequate or a bad one.

Firstly, the museum must have a clear purpose. It needs to be clear to visitors what the museum is 'about'. Ask yourself what stories, or whose stories, it is telling. Most importantly of all, who is it telling these stories to? Knowing your audience is essential if you want to get their attention.

Once you are clear about who you're talking to, you need to seek out imaginative ways of getting your audience's attention. Visits by school groups and education providers are a major potential market for museums, so how are you going to make your collection interesting to children and young people? Don't make any assumptions about the amount of prior cultural knowledge your visitors are likely to have; instead, think about what short cuts you can provide. You want visitors to step into your story as they walk in the door, and you want to keep them with you every step of their visit.

Thirdly, less is more. Always. Don't overload your audience with information but present small themes in 'layers' within one larger topic. Make any text not only concise but 'skimmable' so that visitors can read it quickly and get the main ideas.

In fourth place, not top of the list, but not far from it, is technology. Having interactive, multi-media presentations is no longer an option – it's an expectation. Visitors to museums are no longer satisfied with just reading labels. You have to find ways to get them to participate in your museum experience. Technology isn't the only way to do this but it will be an essential element in your strategy.

Finally, don't forget the basics. It's surprising how often people do. These include good lighting, clear signposting, clean and adequate toilet facilities and, wherever possible, a great museum shop and café to boost your brand and your revenues. And last of all, great marketing. If you want to attract visitors, they have to know who you are and where to find you.

6.3

1 a carved jade figure of a horse
2 a flint knife with an ivory handle
3 a silver mirror decorated with amber
4 an antique leather writing case
5 over three hundred and fifty Chinese ink paintings
6 fragments of a painted plaster ceiling
7 Viking cooking utensils
8 an immense brown earthenware vase

Unit 7

7.1

O = Olga, A = Anke

O So, Anke, we all know it wasn't a great success, but let's have a look together at what went wrong, and why it did.

A Well, the first problem was the venue. It was cheaper than the alternatives in the city centre, but it was just horrible. It's one of those 60s concrete buildings, very ugly inside and out and, since it was off the ring road outside the city, impossible to get to except by car. The only way for the delegates to get into town was by taking an expensive taxi.

O Did the clients think about providing a shuttle bus?

A They rejected the suggestion as too expensive. Basically, the clients had unrealistic expectations from the beginning about the overall cost of running a conference and this caused lots of problems. But the biggest issue was that it was impossible to find your way round the building. The layout is very complicated and very badly signposted. As a result, people got lost all the time, so they missed the sessions they wanted to go to or arrived very late. It put everyone in a bad temper. We had meant to put up extra signs but we just didn't have time. What made it worse was that the map provided in the delegates' conference pack was upside down! It was the one the centre had given us, so the mistake originated with them and we didn't check it, and we didn't notice the problem until we'd printed 600 of them!

O And I gather there was a problem with the catering facilities as well?

A Yes, the kitchen and dining facilities were totally inadequate for the size of the building and number of delegates. It took over two hours to serve everyone lunch on the first day and the queues were enormous. The food wasn't bad but it was only free for exhibitors and speakers – the ordinary delegates had to pay, which was another source of complaint, especially as the food was quite expensive. I think this was another big mistake because actually a set lunch wouldn't have cost them much per head, and free food creates a lot of goodwill.

7.2

1 He wouldn't have done it if he had known better.
2 How long have you had this problem?
3 They haven't finished, have they?
4 If they had arrived earlier, we would have started by now.
5 I don't think they had ever discussed it, had they?

7.3

A = Anke, O = Olga

A I still can't believe these clients are prepared to spend so much money. Where does it all come from?

O Well, Taylor Lehmann makes milllions from all of her films and as for Victor Londretti, who knows what footballers get paid now? It *is* a great thing for us to get such a high-value contract, but I wish they hadn't decided to do it in India when most of the guests are American or European. And I especially wish we had more time! The logistics involved in flying all the guests out and home again is going to be challenging.

A I think we need a special task force, especially to deal with guest transport. I was going to ask Geeta, the new intern, to take it on. Her family comes from India, so she's probably quite good at the geography.

O OK, good idea – as long as Geeta doesn't mind being a task force by herself! There are 215 guests, from all over the world, so she'd better get going …

A Definitely!

O OK, as your particular responsibility is the reception party, I wanted to update you on the latest. I was very firm with Taylor yesterday and told her she really can't change her mind anymore or we're going to run out of time. She's now definitely decided that she and Victor are going to make their entrance to the palace courtyard where the wedding ceremony will be, riding on elephants, so I'll confirm that with Raj at Ranthambore so he can set things in motion for the elephant hire. We need two for the wedding ceremony, and those plus four more for the reception procession.

A Are you serious?

O Absolutely, and since the dates of the wedding coincide with a big local festival, the local elephants are apparently going to be very much in demand. We need to have a contingency plan to source them from further afield if necessary.

A Has Taylor finally made up her mind about the entertainment for the reception as well? I need to start coordinating between the two agencies in Mumbai where we're getting the Bollywood dancers and the entertainers from.

O Um, well, I'm afraid Victor wants some fire-eaters now, as well.

A Oh dear, fire. Could that be outside? Otherwise I think we might have to change the insurance contract for the hire of the marquees for the reception. They've all got wooden floors, you know. I know they said a budget of three million dollars, but the reception costs seem to double every time someone has a conversation with Taylor!

Unit 8

8.1

A = Alison, Y = Yusef

A My pay is OK, about average for the job, but I'm certainly not earning big bucks like you do!

Y Actually, my basic annual salary isn't great, but in a good year, I can easily double it in sales commissions. I don't think that's going to be the case this year, though, as we've just lost a big customer: another chain has offered them conditions we can't possibly match. That's the problem with performance-related pay. Your work is measured by results, not by the effort you've put in!

A Does your company offer you any fringe benefits, like private health insurance or incentive travel or anything?

Y Not really, unless you count the company car. But since driving is so much part of the job, I don't really think of it in those terms. However, the company's retirement savings scheme is very good. If I stayed in this job for the next 30 years, I'd get an excellent pension at the end of it. I can't imagine doing that, though!

A Well, I can stay at any other Elliott Hotel in the world for at least a 50% discount and I get subsidized membership of Aqua Leisure Clubs because they're in the same group. When I was made a junior manager, I was offered stock options as well, which is great. And it's clever of the hotel, too, because now I feel I've got even more of an interest in making sure the business is a success.

8.2

1 Well, I hope they would say that I'm hard-working and reliable. Yes, and also that I'm a positive person with an upbeat attitude to life. In the past, several people have commented that I'm a good people person. In general, I'm good at getting on with all sorts of different people.

2 I did an internship with a hotel chain in Spain straight after finishing my degree. I mainly worked on the front desk so had a lot of contact with the guests – not just for check-ins and check-outs, but helping them with all the different aspects of their stay. After that, I worked for an educational tour company, leading bus tours through Europe with American high-school students. That was challenging, as the hours were long and being in charge of minors was a lot of responsibility, but I loved it.

3 Well, first of all, I feel it's a natural progression for me in terms of my skills and experience. I mean, my previous jobs will have prepared me well for this one. I can apply all that I have learned about customer service in hotels and as a junior tour leader and develop those skills. But what especially appeals to me is the opportunity to apply these in adventure tourism, which has been my particular passion. Being part of the team that introduces clients to white-water rafting and canoeing would be really exciting.

4 Well, the tour company had some cash-flow problems at one point and since they hadn't paid the coach company, the coach didn't turn up for the final airport transfer. I suddenly found myself having to organize alternative transport to the airport for 60 people at four in the morning. They weren't very happy about it, and one of the teachers started having a panic attack at the thought of missing her flight home, but I managed to get them all on to their flights on time. I got a lot of positive comments in the feedback questionnaires about how I managed that situation.

8.3

G = Greg, M = Melanie

G An interesting morning.

M Absolutely! I can't believe some of the candidates today! What about the guy in the shorts?

G And how many were there that couldn't actually speak English? It's all very well getting someone else to write your resumé for you, but you are going to get found out pretty quickly if you just can't communicate. It's just a waste of everyone's time.

M I don't know, Greg, you've got to admire the courage of people in that situation. Apart from his problems with English, that first candidate, the Chinese man, was very strong.

G Well, OK, but the ad does clearly say fluent English. But let's look at the candidates who actually meet *all* the requirements. I quite liked David Bowden. Let's see, he's had two years' experience in a more junior role at the Carlton in Monte Carlo.

M He seemed very young. Yes, see? He's only 28. A local kid, grew up right here in California. He looked good – although the suit was a bit flashy. He's got a hospitality management degree from Stanford and gave some sharp answers. He's obviously very ambitious, but I'm just not sure he's quite got the maturity to handle the responsibility yet. Particularly with regard to some of the staffing issues. What about the second to last candidate, Jennie Chan?

G Yes, now she was impressive. A real power dresser. She's spent five years with Klimpton Hotels here and in LA and is looking to move up to the next level.

M She had some very interesting things to say about customer service satisfaction and loyalty to the hotel brand. In fact, she said she was a member of the Institute of Customer Service. Very well informed. She's got a degree, hasn't she?

G No, actually, she hasn't. She's got a Diploma in Hospitality Management from London, England. But she did seem very driven. That's the sort of attitude we're looking for.

M And the other one I thought has potential was Pedro Gomez. He's completely bilingual and speaks fluent

Portuguese as well. He's also got a Master's in Hotel Management and two years' experience in a similar job with Seasons Hotel in Mexico City.

G Yes, claims he was headhunted for that position. So, why's he applying for a job with us? I found him a bit arrogant to be honest, and I'm not sure that his managerial style would work with our team.

M He said he's relocating back to the States with his American wife, remember, but I completely agree with you about the people management issue.

G Well, I think we've reached our decision, then. Our second interview shortlist is, well, just Jennie Chan.

8.4

1 We need to advertise this job. Let's put an advertisement on Google.

2 I'm going to refer to the people who you said would give you references.

3 I got a pay increase last year, but I don't think they're going to increase it again soon!

4 If the economy contracts any more, I'll never get a full-time contract.

5 It's an export company, but I don't know exactly what they export.

Unit 9

9.1

The World Tourism Organization classifies culinary tourism as a branch of cultural tourism. This is because people often see the food and drink of the local people as a doorway into the culture of the place they're visiting. Learning to cook on holiday isn't like cooking at home: if you're preparing new types of food in different ways, the whole experience can feel like an adventure. Besides, art and architecture are all very well, but food and drink can offer a much more intense experience. Eating and drinking involve all five of the human senses, so people tend to remember a meal, especially if they have cooked it themselves, much longer than they do a museum or a painting!

I think offering more culinary tours is a natural step for us. According to my research, clients who take culinary vacations tend to be well-educated, affluent professionals. What's important for us is that this is the same customer profile as for the art and culture tours we already specialize in! In this social segment, where everyone has a career and goes out to work, no one has time to cook anymore and cooking is becoming a bit of a lost art. These people are beginning to feel that cooking is something missing from their lives, and growing numbers of them are becoming interested in learning to cook delicious food.

This goes with another social trend, which is the increasing interest in healthy living.

People want to eat fresh, local, organic and seasonal produce and are rediscovering the value of traditional methods of food production and preparation. Although these kinds of values have only quite recently become fashionable, they are exactly what our Italian 'slow food' movement is based on! I see a lot of potential to combine our tours with, for example, visits to organic farms. We could also take in traditional artisan food producers, such as cheese makers and bakers.

I think we should take our existing 'Gastronomic Tuscany' tour as a model, but also differentiate from it. For example, the 'Amalfi Coast' walking tour could become a culinary walking tour, with more of a foodie emphasis. And the 'Three Renaissance Cities' tour could stay more cultural, but we could add, say, a day learning about Renaissance cooking, with a Renaissance-style dinner in the evening to make it more memorable.

9.2

The main reason why so many new restaurants fail is because the owners don't accumulate enough capital before starting their restaurant. So make sure you are realistic about this. Apply for bank loans and business grants to collect money and get as much investment as you can. If you are buying an existing restaurant or other eatery, a blanket price may cover most of the start-up costs, such as industrial kitchen equipment, freezers, tables, shelving, counters, seating for the customers, etc.

Starting from scratch will probably cost you between 100,000 and 300,000 dollars depending on the size and scale of your operation. Calculate these costs carefully and do *not* underestimate them.

The second main cause of failure is that the restaurant concept doesn't meet local needs. Again, it's partly a question of being realistic – for example, an expensive upscale steak house is unlikely to succeed in a poor neighbourhood where there are a lot of vegetarians!

Never start a restaurant unless you're sure you have 'the big three' – a great chef, a great location and a great concept. So, starting with the concept, well, it goes back to what I said before – follow your heart because you've got to believe in what you're doing, but also it's vital to do your research and be realistic. For example, if the current trend is for healthy eating, put some healthy options on your menu. Make sure your pricing is accessible for the local population.

And as far as location is concerned, remember that if your establishment is not located in an area where a lot of people regularly pass through, preferably on foot, you are putting yourself at a tremendous disadvantage. Location is still relevant once you've got customers inside your restaurant, because you've got to make

sure it's a place they feel good in and where they want to stay. For this, every detail counts – from the shining clean cutlery, to the colour of the tablecloths, to the lighting, to the service.

And finally, of course you need your great chef and a great kitchen and dining service team to support him or her. Restaurant managers tend to get obsessed with systems, and it's true that it's essential to have these in place for everything to be running smoothly – from seating the customers quickly to getting their orders on the table. But I find it depressing when I see people putting lots and lots of energy and effort into delivering food that is ultimately mediocre. Never forget that however smooth and polished the service is, in the end a restaurant stands or falls on the passion of everyone that works there for creating great food.

9.3

appraisal improvement solution accessible accumulate constructively conversation disadvantage mediocre

9.4

P = Pablo, E = Enrique

P These critics don't understand anything! They don't understand how hard we work, Enrique!

E But she's said some of the stuff I've been trying to say to you for ages, Papa. You just wouldn't listen.

P I don't remember you saying anything.

E Don't remember, or don't *want* to remember? Come on, this could be the incentive we need to turn things around. You know that profits have fallen badly this last year. We need to improve things to get back on track.

P That's just it. Profits have fallen, so we have no money to change things.

E Then it'll just become a vicious circle and keep getting worse. And you sometimes have to spend money to make money. Let's look at things we can address with the minimum financial input to begin with.

P OK, OK …

E Well, for a start, we could just turn off some of the lights and replace them with candles on the tables. That would create a much cosier and more intimate atmosphere. And a friend of mine is at art college. Maybe we could get him to paint a cactus on the window and a new sign. We could have something modern and funky-looking in a desert setting – and chuck out that mouldy old plastic cactus, which I've wanted to do for years.

P Hey! That cactus has been in my restaurants for over 20 years!

E All the more reason to get rid of it.

P Well … you might be right.

E I am. I know I am. And, for the food … I think it might be time we got Granny out of the kitchen.

P Do you have any idea of what you're asking me to do?

E But her eyesight is getting bad, and her tortillas are so tough because she's putting in too much flour, and forgetting to add the seasonings. Besides, she and José keep having the most terrible fights. That's why the service was so slow on the day the reviewer was here. It was so embarrassing. You could hear them shouting at each other from the dining room. She's spent so many years working in the kitchen – why can't she work in the front of house for a change, helping me to greet and seat the customers? Her Spanish accent is still very strong – it would give a real authentic feel to the place.

P Hmm, I'm not so sure …

E Come on, Papa, you know that José has been threatening to leave if he can't have the kitchen to himself. And then what would we do? We'd never find another chef as good as he is.

P All right, son. I've known deep down we had to make some changes. But will you do me a favour? Will you be the one to tell Granny?

Unit 10

10.1

To be fair, one of the main reasons low-cost operations are a high-risk business and one of the main reasons why Lotta Air failed was due to rises in fuel prices. Many of the more successful budget operations are branches of bigger airlines which can spread the risk of fluctuations in fuel prices by raising the price of their premium fares. However, if you're competing on price alone, of course you can't afford to do this. Lotta also relied too much on technology to replace people for its customer service and didn't take into account that even technology needs a certain level of support. By making the internet not just the primary but, in most cases, the only means of contact with its customers, Lotta Air was taking a risk on the high performance of its badly under-supported computer systems. Of course, problems did occur and they were made worse by the fact that their customers could not talk to anyone directly when this happened. Considering the high quality of service offered by many of their competitors, Lotta also took yet another risk by not investing in recruiting and training high-quality personnel. It hired young college graduates whose primary job, it seemed, was to tell arriving passengers to use the self-check-in machines, and the level of customer care they offered tended to be indifferent at best. The consequence of all this was that despite the competitive cost of their fares, Lotta Air never managed to secure customer loyalty. Many passengers often only flew with them once and the company failed within less than 18 months of starting up.

10.2

1 They can't have (can't've) seen the crash occur.

2 They may have (may've) managed to escape.

3 People shouldn't have (shouldn't've) ignored the safety instructions.

4 The ship may not have (may not've) been able to turn in time.

5 They couldn't have (couldn't've) had much chance of survival in those temperatures.

6 They should have (should've) held an emergency drill as soon as you arrived.

10.3

The *Titanic* sank in the Atlantic Ocean in 1912 with the loss of over 1,500 lives. The ship had been built with the latest technology and was thought to be unsinkable. Because of this, she was only supplied with half the necessary number of lifeboats, as the engineers thought they would never be needed. Most of the sailors on the *Titanic* were recruited the week before the ship sailed and were never given any safety training in the use of lifeboats.

When the iceberg was finally spotted, the Captain was told and he gave the order to change direction. However, the *Titanic* used a different steering system to traditional sailing ships of the time, and the helmsman, the person steering the ship, got confused. He directed the ship towards the iceberg, not away from it. By the time this mistake had been realized, the ship was going too fast to change direction in time to avoid a collision.

Tragically, many of the lifeboats that left the sinking ship were only half full as no one really knew how many people could fit into them. The people who jumped into the freezing water died quickly from exposure. Of the survivors, very few were third-class passengers, who were accommodated in the lower part of the ship, below the water line, and had a locked gate to keep them separate from the first- and second-class ticket holders. This gate was reputedly never unlocked in the panic as the ship went down.

As the stricken ship started taking in water, it should have stopped. Instead, it was ordered to keep moving so that it wouldn't sink in the middle of the Atlantic, and this movement caused water to enter the ship even more quickly. The ship broke into two pieces and sank to the sea bed, some 4,000 metres below the surface.

Pearson Education Limited
Edinburgh Gate
Harlow
Essex CM20 2JE
England
and Associated Companies throughout the world.

www.pearsonelt.com/tourism

First published 2013

ISBN: Workbook +Key/Audio CD Pk
9781447923930
Printed by Neografia in Slovakia

Workbook -Key/Audio CD Pk
9781447923947
Printed and bound by CPI Group (UK) Ltd, Croydon, CR0 4YY

Set in Avenir Light 9.5/12.5pt

We are grateful to the following for permission to reproduce copyright material:

Tables
Table Unit1.1 adapted from http://www.nationmaster.com/graph/eco_tou_arr_by_reg_of_ori_eur-tourist-arrivals-region-origin-europe, World Tourism Organization Statistics Database and Yearbook | United Nations World Tourism Organization; Table Unit1.3 adapted from http://www.statcan.gc.ca/tables-tableaux/sum-som/l01/cst01/arts34-eng.htm

Text
Article Unit1.2 adapted from http://www.tourism.australia.com/en-au/research/5236_6563.aspx, Tourism Australia; Article Unit5. adapted from www.terminalu.com/editors-column/what-makes-a-good-airport-and-why-many-have-got-it-wrong/15594/, Louise Driscoll; Extract Unit5.6 adapted from http://www.iom-airport.com/customer/safety.xml, Isle of Man Government ©2012 Crown Copyright

In some instances we have been unable to trace the owners of copyright material, and we would appreciate any information that would enable us to do so.

'DK' and the DK 'open book' logo are trade marks of Dorling Kindersley Limited and are used in this publication under licence.

Picture Credits
The publisher would like to thank the following for their kind permission to reproduce their photographs:

(Key: b-bottom; c-centre; l-left; r-right; t-top)

Alamy Images: Leonelolo Calvetti 13, Blaine Harrington III 31, Lordprice Collection 43, David Pearson 23, John Warburton-Lee Photography 25; **Corbis:** 21-23tr; **Digital Vision:** 19; **DK Images:** Jamie Marshall 7t; **Fotolia.com:** Yuri Arcurs 29-31tr, arrow 8-10tl, germanskydive110 40-42tl, Macropixel 17-19tr, Erica Guilane-Nachez 4-6tl, 5-7tr, Think4photop 16-18tl, Leah-Anne Thompson 36-38tl; **Imagestate Media:** John Foxx Collection 33; **John Foxx Images:** 41-43tr; **MIXA Co Ltd:** 35r; **Pearson Education Ltd:** Jon Barlow 33-35tr, Jules Selmes 24-26tl; **Peter Evans:** 26; **PhotoDisc:** 37-39tr, Jackson Vereen / Cole Publishing Group 36, Andrew Ward / Life File 24; **Shutterstock.com:** Arcardy 40, bumihills 37, chert28 22, Francesco Dazzi 16, Denphumi 9-11tr, EpicStockMedia 41, Jeffrey M. Frank 39, jakobradlgruber 8, jbor 13-15tr, Stuart Jenner 9, Morgan Lane Photography 5t, Vitalii Nesterchuk 32-34tl, Olga A 25-27tr, oliveromg 11, Tyler Olsen 21, Carlos Restrepo 20-22tl, ruigsantos 34, Stefanolunardi 12-14tl, Mark Yuill 28-30tl; **www.imagesource.com:** 35b, Carl Glover 35l

Cover images: Front: **4Corners Images:** Guido Cozzi / SIME bc, Massimo Ripani / SIME tc; **Corbis:** Blaine Harrington III b; **Getty Images:** Stuart Westmorland t; Back: DK Images: Greg Ward bl; **Robert Harding World Imagery:** Mark Mawson tl; **Shutterstock.com:** Yuri Yavnik cl

All other images © Pearson Education

In some instances we have been unable to trace the owners of copyright material, and we would appreciate any information that would enable us to do so.